# Country Property
## *Dirt Cheap*

RALPH C. TURNER

# Country Property

## *Dirt Cheap*

How I Found My Piece of
Inexpensive Rural Land...
Plus My Adventures with
a $300 ~~Junk~~ *Antique* Tractor

# RALPH C. TURNER

INDEX LEGALIS PUBLISHING COMPANY, INC.
FAIRFIELD, IOWA

To my father
for his love and support

# Country Property Dirt Cheap
## How I Found My Piece of Inexpensive Rural Land
Plus My Adventures With a $300 ~~Junk~~ *Antique* Tractor

Copyright © 1996 by Ralph C. Turner

Printed and bound in the United States of America

Published by
Index Legalis Publishing Company, Inc.
Post Office Box 1822-5
Fairfield, IA 52556
(641) 472-2293

### Library of Congress Cataloging-in-Publication Data

Turner, Ralph C., 1943-
    Country property dirt cheap: how I found my piece of
inexpensive rural land plus my adventures with a $300
junk/antique tractor / by Ralph C. Turner
        p.   cm.
    Includes index.
    ISBN 0-945959-52-4
    1. Real property--Purchasing. 2. Country homes--Purchasing.
3. Real property--Iowa--Purchasing--Case studies. 4. Country
homes--Iowa--Purchasing--Case studies. 5. House buying--Iowa--
Case studies.  I. Title.
HD1379.T84   1996
333.33'53--dc20                                    95-19237

# CONTENTS

5

# FOREWORD

This is a warm, funny story about a man with a dream – a dream of owning a bit of country land.

With only $6,000 in hand, and discouraged by real estate brokers who quote $20,000 as a minimum, he decides to go for it on his own. In the process, the author, Ralph Turner, meets delightful rural characters and discovers how to hunt down potential sellers and get around their reluctance to break off and sell a small piece of land.

For his $6,000 he ends up with fifteen beautiful wooded acres where he can camp, hike, and eventually build a home.

For $300 he acquires an ancient tractor which creates some exciting episodes as it acquires the temperament of a life-threatening rogue stallion.

For another $100 he buys a 10x14-foot sleeping cabin. The only problem – it's fourteen miles on rustic rural roads from his recently acquired property. Unable to afford professional house movers, he has to tackle the job himself, which gives rise to further adventures.

The reader will come to the conclusion that if Ralph Turner can become the equivalent of a country squire, anyone can do it.

Although this is not a "how to" book as such, anyone who opens these pages will find valuable down-to-earth search and investigative techniques. In short, this is a good book for both the armchair and the practical dreamer.

GERALD L. FREEMAN

# INTRODUCTION

When I told a friend of mine that I was writing a book about buying inexpensive rural property, she challenged me with a question. "How can such a book be useful to anyone living outside your own state of Iowa? Here in California where I live, you'd never be able to find a bargain like the one you unearthed in the Midwest."

It's true that property values vary drastically from region to region. According to recent statistics, for example, the average per-acre value of farmland and buildings in Wyoming was $169, compared with $4,840 in New Jersey. (In Iowa, the average was $1,316.)* Despite such geographical disparities, though, you should be able to find a piece of property in your own area at a bargain price, *relative to the price of other parcels in your own area.*

The truth is, it doesn't matter what state or province you live in. If you're willing to do some sleuthing, and if you know how to follow through on the leads you uncover, you can dramatically increase your chances of finding a great piece of country property at a relatively low price, regardless of where you live. This holds true whether you're interested in finding a small farm, a summer cottage on a lake, a mountain retreat with a cabin, or just an isolated parcel of woodland to hike or hunt on.

It also doesn't matter at what point in time you're looking for property. Although land prices may go up (or down) from year to year, bargains can always be found, provided you're willing to do some work to uncover them.

* Source: U.S. Dept. of Agriculture, Economic Research Service, *Agricultural Resources, Agricultural Land Values and Markets, Situation and Outlook Report,* annual.

My own search turned out to be more complicated than I had expected. I discovered that it was hard to find a rural acreage at a good price through a real estate agent. That meant I had to hunt down potential sellers on my own. I came up with eighteen methods of doing this.

Then another problem surfaced. I found that farmers (and other rural property owners) don't usually want to break off and sell a small piece of real estate. There are a number of reasons for this, and more than one way to get around the problem.

The process of hunting down owners and evaluating different parcels of land was an education in itself. I learned about property values, deeds, land surveys, special types of maps, real estate auctions, surplus government land, and tax sales, among other things.

Far from being tedious, the search proved to be exciting. Every time I explored a deserted barn, or walked the fence line of a timbered parcel, I found myself drawn more and more to the peaceful quiet of the back country.

Eventually, I found and bought a small piece of rural property. It's a breathtakingly beautiful place, and, as you'll see, I was able to buy it at a surprisingly low price.

Soon after I purchased the land, I realized that other people might be interested in reading about the steps I had taken to hunt down property. Initially, I considered writing the book in the form of a "how-to" manual, but most of the how-to manuals I had read over the years reminded me of boring high school textbooks.

So instead, I decided to write this book as a first person account. Not only will it be easier and more fun to read, but the narrative format will lend itself to what this really is: the story of a series of experiences, each one of which taught me something about buying rural property.

In the first part of the book, I describe the methods I used to track down properties. Then I tell about the piece of land I eventually purchased. It's all one story, though, since each false start played an important role in leading to my ultimate success.

What follows is the account of my adventure, an adventure full of back road explorations, courthouse searches, colorful property owners, my experiences with a $300 antique farm tractor, and the acquisition of a $100 cabin.

Although I've used fictitious names for people and places, the whole account is true, including the unusual events.

## CHAPTER ONE

# MY FIRST
# NEWSPAPER ADVERTISEMENT

ON- 4x4, automatic, les, runs 375. Call 672.

88 Jeep 4x4 AC Automatic. 00 or best -4735.

RUCK- 5

great room ... kitchen, fireplace, walk-in closets, city water, completely remodeled. Call after 6 p.m. 555-2428.

WANTED TO BUY: Barn or garage (can need repairs) on small rural acreage in Columbia County. Call after 7 p.m., 555-2293

BUILDING LOT - For sale, level, 1.8 miles southeast city, great views, large

Baker, ow, auctioneer.

SUNDAY, A Real estat Block 6, Dalton, low home hook' shed and Located 1 bl. evevator in Dennebeim. Peters A Springfield

It was three months after I had started my search for property. I had put a lot of effort into writing the ad, choosing and rearranging each word carefully, and I had visions of my phone, if not exactly ringing off the hook, at least keeping me busy with responses. After all, you don't have to drive down too many gravel or dirt roads in Columbia County, Iowa, before you come across at least one old barn.

My ad ran for twelve days in the *Springfield Gazette*, the only daily newspaper in this agricultural county in southern Iowa, thirty miles north of the Missouri state line.

I got two responses from the ad.

The first call was from a farmer who had a barn to sell, without land. He said I could move the barn off his property, or tear it down for the lumber. Buying a building seemed premature, though, since I wasn't a land owner yet.

About a week later I received the only other response to the ad. This call was from a man who sounded as if he was in his thirties.

> *Caller:* I own an old one-room schoolhouse that I might be willing to sell. It's on a third of an acre.
>
> *Me:* Oh... well... I'm actually looking for land with a barn on it, or some place where I can store a tractor. But I'd still like to take a look. Do you know how much you want for it?
>
> *Caller:* Yes.

14

*Me:* ...uh, how much?

*Caller:* That's my business. You tell me how much you'll give.

The property was twenty miles out of town, and since he didn't own a car, we made arrangements for me to pick him up. When I arrived at his house he was standing in the front yard waiting for me. I reached over and opened the passenger door of my car, but instead of getting in, he said, "Before we go any further, you should know that I won't accept anything less than $5,000."

I tried to keep a straight face, since I had no intention of paying that much for one-third of an acre. However, I was still interested in looking at the property. During the drive out, he told me he had bought the schoolhouse at an auction.

His land, which abutted a gravel road, was on flat countryside surrounded by cornfields. There were no trees. Part of the roof of the schoolhouse had fallen in, apparently years ago, and the moment I saw its rotting timbers and barren setting, I realized I didn't want the property, even if he would come down on the price.

While riding in the car back to Springfield, I told him that I'd have to think about it. As I drove away from his house, I became discouraged. The newspaper ad hadn't produced a single suitable lead, and here was someone asking $5,000 for a third of an acre with a useless building on it.

Of course, I *had* found out one thing. I had learned that my ad was worded so poorly that the farmer thought I was looking for a barn to tear down, rather than a piece of land to buy.

But I'm getting ahead of myself. You really should know why I was looking for a piece of country property, and why I wanted a place to store a tractor.

I guess it all started about forty-six years ago with a little boy's dream.

## CHAPTER TWO

# THE
# UNFULFILLED DREAM

When I was about six years old I started dreaming about Jeeps and tractors and candy bars.

Sometimes the images came during the middle of the night, sometimes they were in the form of daydreams. The mental picture that brought me the most pleasure was of a Jeep whose glove compartment was stuffed with Snickers bars.

I wanted a real Jeep and a real tractor, but all I could afford were Snickers bars. I never even got to ride in a Jeep, or so much as sit on a tractor's seat. As soon as I got my first bicycle, I forgot all about the dreams.

Home was in Schenectady, New York, about half way between New York City and Canada. I lived with my parents and brother in a modest house on a tree-lined street. Dad was a newspaper editorial writer.

Our summers were spent in a rented cottage on the shore of Lake George, in the Adirondack mountains. Although there were dirt roads and footpaths near the camp, I liked best to strike out into the woods where there were no trails. It was during those solitary wanderings up on the mountains, among the trees and along the streams, that I first realized I loved to be alone.

One day, near the end of the summer of my fourteenth year, I headed into the woods in a new direction. After walking a couple of miles I came upon an abandoned church. Years before, a tiny hamlet had grown up there. But now, the church was all that remained.

One of the doors of the building had fallen off, and I stepped inside. An old pump organ sat to the side of the pulpit, and Bibles and hymnals were still tucked into their racks on the backs of the pews. The floor was covered with leaves blown in by the wind, and it looked as if years had passed since the church had been used.

Tired from the hike, I lay down on the floor to rest. I could hear the wind whistling through the trees which surrounded and sheltered the church. I felt content, and my thoughts were peaceful:

*This is the most beautiful spot in the world.*

I returned to the church a number of times that summer, but soon, vacation was over. The following year I got a summer job at a different part of the lake, and I wasn't able to visit the abandoned church again. The memory of that building, however, remained with me and became my new fantasy.

No matter where I was for the next few years, the thought of that deserted church, isolated and among the high trees, brought me a measure of peace. When I was troubled and had difficulty falling asleep, it was that building that my mind would return to.

The dream grew. As I lay in bed waiting for sleep to come, I saw not only the church, peaceful and private, but I also saw myself owning it. That deserted building would someday be my retreat where I could go anytime I wanted.

More years went by. I went off to college, moved out on my own, then got a job. Suddenly, there were no more summers. It was just work, one week after the other.

Sometime during the passage from young man to adult, the peaceful dreams of that deserted church had faded away. Maybe the dreams died because, now that I was mature and sensible, they seemed unattainable. After all, I wasn't rich, and buying a building in the country seemed extravagant. As the years passed by, I even came to feel that walks in the woods were a waste of time. They were unproductive.

Then in 1991, at age forty-eight, something unexpected happened.

A thought of death came.

CHAPTER THREE

# THE
# VISION

My parents and I had moved to Springfield, a town in southern Iowa with a population of about 8,000. Mom was eighty-six, Dad eighty-four, and their health was failing. I tried not to think of the inevitability of their passing away, but it was impossible not to worry. Sometimes I would leave their house and wander the streets, trying (possibly) to exercise away my sadness and feeling of helplessness.

Once, as I walked down the middle of the street at four in the morning, the darkness beautiful, a thought of death came.

*I could die at any moment.*

I stopped walking, and more thoughts came.

*If I discovered I had only one more year to live, and I could do anything I wanted, anything at all, what would I do?*

In answer, a series of images unfolded before me, half visual, half dream:

I saw myself sitting on a farm tractor, pulling logs out of the woods. I drove the tractor into an old barn. The tractor and the barn and the woods were mine.

CHAPTER FOUR

# DECISION

I was a writer of technical books about computers. Being self-employed meant that I could arrange the day's activities to my liking, taking time off whenever I wanted.

Instead, I was a workaholic. I worked mornings, afternoons, and evenings, seven days a week. Even when I was in the bathtub, I had a pencil and paper with me so I could continue working.

The idea of pursuing the dream seemed like the perfect change. But it frightened me. I was afraid that acting on it would be a financial mistake, as well as a waste of time. After all, I certainly didn't *need* a tractor or a piece of country property.

*But if I don't follow the dream, I'll regret it for the rest of my life.*

I pictured myself an old man confined to his bed, never having driven a tractor.

*I'm going to do it!*

\* \* \* \*

A few days later, while glancing through *The Weekly Shopper*, Springfield's free weekly advertising throwaway, I saw an ad which immediately got me excited.

## Chapter Five

# THE
# RIVER CABIN

in Blair County, older
farmhouse and 50 acres
with approx. 40 acres
tillable, remainder in
pasture and timber, low
70's. 555-2428.

FOR SALE: Cabin on Rock
River near Burnt Hills.
$5,000. Call 555-1765

HOUSE FOR SALE: three
bedroom ranch on 4.5
acres with pond and 36X52
pole garage. Beautiful

When I called the telephone number listed in the ad, an elderly lady answered. The property, she said, was near the town of Burnt Hills, below Springfield in Fillmore County. The cabin, which had electricity but no running water, was on a plot that was 200 feet wide by 50 feet deep.

"Go take a look," she said. "If you like it, I'll come down and show you the inside of the cabin. Oh, by the way... there ain't no abstract, and I'll give you a quit claim deed." *

During the 20-mile drive south I could barely contain my excitement. A cabin on a river for only $5,000! In my mind's eye I saw a rustic log cabin perched on top of a hill overlooking the river, surrounded by trees and outcroppings of bedrock. Maybe there would even be a barn or a shed where I could store a tractor.

Burnt Hills consisted of five old wood-frame houses clustered next to the river on flat land. The cabin was on the outskirts of town on a small strip of land lying between the river and a one-lane gravel road that ran parallel to the river. The Rock River is about 800 feet wide at that point.

When I stepped out of my air conditioned car on that humid July afternoon, the ninety-five degree heat reminded me of how much I disliked hot weather. There was a breeze, though, blowing in across the water, and as the cool air struck my face, I thought:

*What a beautiful spot. This is the kind of place I want, a place on the water.*

The cabin, which was one story high, had roughly the square footage of a two-car garage. It sat on piers sunk in the river bank about ten feet in from the water's edge. I tried to look through the windows, but they were covered up from the inside.

* Iowa is one of the states where an Abstract of Title is relied on as proof that the seller holds clear title to the property, and can thus convey the property to the buyer free of any liens. At the other extreme are states that rely solely on insurance as a means of protecting a buyer. Many other states use a combination of these two systems. The Abstract, which is compiled by an abstract company, is a history of everyone who has owned the property in the past. (The Abstract also lists all encumbrances and liens affecting the title to the property.) The seller pays the abstract company to prepare an up-to-date continuation of the Abstract of Title, which is turned over to the buyer's attorney for examination and then given to the buyer at the closing.

The seller also gives the buyer a deed, which transfers title to the property. There are a number of types of deeds, the most desirable (from the buyer's standpoint) being the warranty deed. In this type of deed, the seller guarantees

23

The cabin was shaded by two large oak trees and a number of smaller evergreens. The river was beautiful, and the breeze was soothing.

An old flat-bottom rowboat was floating in the water, tied up to a tree stump. I sat down on the river bank and wondered what it would be like to own the property. I could buy a sail boat and explore the river, and at night when I was in bed, I would hear the rippling of the water against the shore as I drifted off to sleep.

During the drive back home I decided to talk to Chuck, a friend of mine, about the quit claim deed and the lack of an abstract. I often went to him when I was unsure about something, or when I needed someone to bounce an idea off. He was about my age, and over the years he had held so many different types of jobs that he seemed to know a little bit about everything.

that clear title is being conveyed. (This guarantee can be sued upon, assuming the buyer can find the seller.)

A quit claim deed conveys only whatever interest the seller *may* have in a piece of property, but no assurances are made as to what that interest might be. With a quit claim deed, the only thing the seller is saying is, "Whatever interest I have in this property, I transfer that interest to you." A quit claim is sometimes used when a husband and wife take title to property, but later get divorced. The husband might then quit claim his interest to his former wife.

*Chuck:* Be careful, Ralph. I've heard that some of the sellers of those parcels down on the river don't hold full title.

*Me:* What do you mean?

*Chuck:* I'm not sure, but something about them having only a 99-year lease.

*Me:* That could be why she wants to use a quit claim.

*Chuck:* Maybe. Quit claims are sometimes used by sellers who own less than complete title to property. But lots of people use them around here, even when they *do* have full title.

*Me:* Why are they so popular?

*Chuck:* Some people think they're simpler. But quit claims don't make sense from the buyer's standpoint, since they're the least desirable kind of deed. Shucks, I could sign a quit claim right now that sells you my interest in the Golden Gate Bridge, and I wouldn't be breaking any law, and I wouldn't be engaging in fraud.

The next day I visited the county health department. I learned that, pursuant to the county's waste water regulations, a sewage treatment system has to be at least 100 feet from any lake or reservoir, and at least twenty-five feet from any stream or open ditch. According to an official in the health department, the Rock River would fall into the same category as a stream.

In other words, the drainage lines from a septic tank would have to be at least twenty-five feet from the river. However, there was an additional requirement that no portion of any treatment system could be closer than ten feet to a property line.

"On a narrow property like that," the health department official said, "one option would be to install a holding tank. Of course, you'd have to get it pumped out periodically. But if you're using the property only in the summer, that might be your best way to go... Oops! I didn't mean to put it *that* way."

Next, I drove over to the courthouse. At the assessor's office I asked the clerk about the 99-year leases.

*Clerk:* Well, some of those river cabins are on land owned by the state. The owners don't really own... you know what I'm saying?

*Me:* You mean they're squatters?

*Clerk:* Right.

*Me:* Have any of the squatters ever tried to sell their cabins?

*Clerk:* Yes, that's happened.

*Me:* What do they do, use a quit claim deed?

*Clerk:* Right.

*Me:* What about the buyers? Have they known that they're buying only the cabin, but no interest in land?

*Clerk:* A few of them were aware of that.

*Me:* But some of the buyers thought they were acquiring an interest in land?

*Clerk:* Yes, unfortunately.

Next, the clerk helped me locate the cabin property on a large aerial photograph. She then gave me the number of the book and the page number where I could find the deed which the owner had received when she acquired the property years ago.

Down the hall at the recorder's office, I used the book and page numbers to locate the deed, which turned out to be a warranty deed. The document, which had been issued by the probate court after the present owner's husband died, established full title in the present owner. I also found an earlier deed. In this document, which transferred title to the present owner and her husband, the original owner guaranteed that he held the property by title "in fee simple." In other words, he was conveying complete and absolute title to the property.

So the question remained: since the present owner held full title to the property, why did she want to use a quit claim deed?

That night I called the owner again, and the next day we met at the cabin. When she stepped out of her car, I noticed that she was wearing a simple print dress which, although clean and ironed, looked like it had been stylish back in the 1950s. She was tall and thin, and she had on a pair of black, lace-up leather shoes that extended up past her ankles.

*Owner:* We bought the place ten years ago, but then Henry passed away.

*Me:* Why do you want to use a quit claim deed?

*Owner:* It's just... you can do it real quick.

*Me:* But it doesn't provide any protection.

*Owner:* I don't know anything about that, but it's just simpler. With a regular deed, you've got to register it.

*Me:* You mean *record* it?

*Owner:* Yes, record it. A quit claim... you can fill that out in five minutes, and you don't have to go through an attorney.*

*Me:* What about the abstract?

---

* After a property is sold, the buyer *records* the deed at the Recorder's Office at the County Courthouse. All deeds, including quit claims, should be recorded. By recording the deed, the buyer prevents the seller from subsequently conveying title to someone else. Additionally, a lien filed against

*Owner:* Oh, that got lost years ago when Henry
and I moved. It shouldn't be too expensive
for you to replace it. *

*Me:* How much did you say you were asking?

*Owner:* Five thousand, just what we paid when we
bought. It's worth more than that, but it
should go to someone who, you know, will
appreciate it. Henry would want that.

I thought she was feeding me a line with her statement about
offering a low price to an appreciative buyer, but even if she was,
I wasn't annoyed. I was anxious to see the inside of the cabin.

The minute we entered the building, any interest I had in the
property vanished. There was something oppressive about the
interior of the cabin, although I couldn't put my finger on what
it was. Something made me uncomfortable, something more
than just the smell of mildew and the sight of the discolored,
rain-damaged ceiling.

The place actually gave me the creeps. I was anxious to get
out of the building, but I didn't have the guts to tell the owner
how I felt, so I said I'd have to think about it, and that I'd get
back to her. That night I called her and explained that, although
the location was beautiful, I was looking for something a little
more isolated.

After we hung up, I got to thinking. What type of property,
exactly, *was* I looking for?

---

the seller (even after the sale of the property) may also become a lien against
the buyer if the buyer has failed to record the deed.

It's always safer to have an attorney handle a land transfer, regardless of the
type of deed used.

* It can, in fact, cost hundreds of dollars to have a new abstract created.

CHAPTER SIX

# WISH LIST

What characteristics, I asked myself, do I want my property to have?  Taking pen in hand, I made the following "wish list" of desirable features:

> secluded rural site
> wooded
> hilly
> $5,000 to $8,000
> next to river or lake
> barn or garage
> scenic views
> good well
> as many acres as possible
> no more than twenty-five miles from
>     my home in Springfield

I realized I might have difficulty finding a piece of property that fulfilled each item on the list, but I hoped to satisfy as many features as possible.

I didn't plan on moving onto the property and residing there permanently.  For one thing, I enjoyed living in Springfield. The town was big enough to have most of the stores I needed, yet small enough that there wasn't a lot of automobile traffic or crime.  Also, I wanted to remain close to my parents in case of an emergency.  Neither mom nor dad could drive a car any more, and I felt more comfortable knowing that if either of them became ill, I'd be close by.

So, rather than wanting property to live on, I was looking for

29

a place for overnight and weekend visits. That's why the spot should be no more than twenty-five miles from home.

Although I was willing to spend $5,000 to $8,000, I had no idea how many acres could be bought for that amount. In fact, I wasn't sure whether *any* land meeting my criteria could be purchased that cheaply.

To get an idea of how many acres I needed, I visited two friends who lived on a farm seven miles out of town. Their four-and-one-half-acre parcel consisted of half pasture and half crop land. They had an old farmhouse, a large barn, and a number of small out buildings. In order to get a feel for how large four-and-one-half acres was, I climbed up to the loft of the barn and looked out the hay window.

I tried to imagine what their property would look like if it was covered with trees and was hilly. I wondered what would happen if, after I had bought such a property, people moved onto the adjacent pieces of land and built homes. Maybe the new neighbors would make lots of noise. Would four-and-one-half acres provide enough of a buffer? I wasn't sure, but I made up my mind that I shouldn't settle for anything less than five acres.

After returning home, I unfolded a road map of Iowa on the kitchen table. I tried to see which towns, roads and parks were within twenty-five miles. The easiest way to visualize this, I found, was to hold a measuring compass on the map.

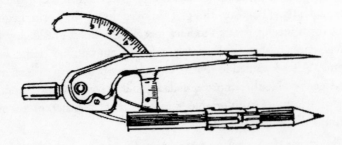

With the point of the instrument positioned on Springfield, I drew a circle that had a radius of twenty-five miles. I decided to refer to the land within the circle as my "target area."

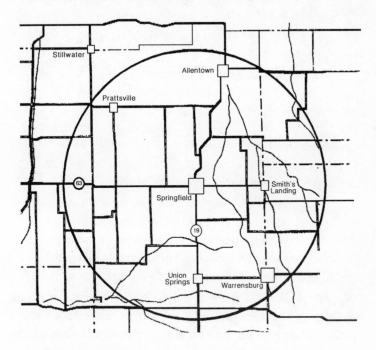

The circle straddled seven counties and contained, according to my calculations, 1,806 square miles. Somewhere in that circle, I felt, there was bound to be a piece of property that would satisfy my wish list.

When I ran into Chuck at the coffee shop a few days later, he was adamant about what I should do next.

## Chapter Seven

# THE
# REAL ESTATE BROKER

*Chuck:* Why don't you just go to a real estate broker?

*Me:* I don't think I'll find anything cheap through a broker.

*Chuck:* Price is determined by supply and demand. Buying property is just a matter of paying the market value. The person who's an expert at helping you is the broker.

I was skeptical. I knew a young married couple that had bought property through a real estate broker. Later, they found a number of comparable properties that they could have bought cheaper on their own.

*Me:* The higher the sales price, the higher the broker's commission. He wants the price as high as possible.

*Chuck:* That's not true. Although he wants a high commission, he also wants a sale. If there's no sale, he doesn't get a commission. It's not in the broker's interest to list a property way over market value.

*Me:* But if I buy directly from the seller, I'll avoid paying the broker's six per cent commission.

*Chuck:* *You* don't pay the commission, the *seller* does.

*Me:* But I *end up* paying it, since the seller invariably computes the amount of the commission into his asking price.

*Chuck:* You'll save yourself a lot of time by using a broker. He knows everybody in the county, and he knows what properties are for sale.

*Me:* I bet there are properties that aren't on the market, but that could be bought.

Chuck sucked in a deep breath, then exhaled slowly and noisily.

*Chuck:* Come on, Ralph. Brokers aren't big, bad people who are trying to gyp you. They're there to help you. Give them a chance. You have nothing to lose.

The conversation got me wondering, and I decided to at least find out if there were any small properties on the market.

The next day I walked into the office of one of the real estate brokers in Springfield. A woman, probably in her sixties, sat behind a desk reading the comic strips in a newspaper.

*Me:* I'm looking for some property in the country. About ten acres, and I'd like some trees. I don't need a house, but it'd be nice if there were a barn on it.

*Broker:* How much are you willing to spend?

*Me:* Umm, maybe $5,000.

*Broker:* Oooh. The days of ten acres at $500 per acre are gone forever. But, let me see... oh, yes. I do have something I can show you, a very nice place. Eleven acres, mostly timber. There's a brook running through it. It's real pretty, and there's some pasture. About twelve miles out of Springfield.

*Me:* How much?

*Broker:* $1,975 per acre.

That amounted to almost $22,000, or about three times what I wanted to spend, so I decided not to even bother looking at the property.

Over the next few days I visited four other brokers. None of them, however, had any inexpensive small acreages. I wasn't discouraged, though, since there was another method of searching for property that I hadn't tried yet.

CHAPTER EIGHT

# READING
# THE NEWSPAPER ADS

Although I had been glancing occasionally at the classified
advertisements in our local paper, I now developed a routine of
methodically checking the ads every day. As soon as the paper
boy pushed the *Springfield Gazette* through the mail slot in the
front door, I'd turn to the real estate section of the ads. I worried
that, if I didn't read the ads as soon as the paper arrived,
somebody else might beat me to the perfect piece of property.

I soon discovered that not many people advertised rural land
for sale. In fact, weeks would sometimes go by during which not
a single listing appeared in the paper's "Real Estate: farms &
lands" section.

Even when rural listings did appear, many of the properties
included farmhouses. Since I wanted to get the greatest number
of acres for a given price, and since I intended to visit the land for
short periods rather than live permanently on it, I didn't want to
pay for a house that I didn't need. Therefore, I concentrated on
finding raw, unimproved land.

Most of the newspaper listings were for large tracts of land:

    240 acres (pasture and timber) $96,000

    120 acres (75 acres tillable) $60,000

    300 acres (120 tillable, balance in timber) $135,000

Occasionally, smaller acerages were advertised:

44 acres (36 timber, 8 tillable) $66,000

23 wooded acres $29,000

After a few weeks of reading the ads, I saw that prices for property followed a pattern. In parcels of 100 or more acres, a price as low as $500 per acre wasn't uncommon. For larger tracts, the price might go as low as $400 per acre. But for parcels with less than twenty-five acres or so, $1,000 or more per acre was often asked. In other words, the greater the number of acres in a parcel, the lower the price per acre.

In the months that followed, I was surprised at how many people were apparently unaware of this rule. One old timer, a farmer who had grown up in New England, told me of the astronomical appreciation in value of Vermont land. When he was a boy, he said, uncleared land near his home could be bought for $50 an acre. But nowadays, he reported, that same land was selling for $5,000 an acre.

When I questioned him about it, he admitted that the $50 per acre price had been for a large parcel of 600 acres, while the $5,000 price per acre was for a parcel of four acres. Although there obviously *had* been a high appreciation, it wasn't as dramatic as he thought. His comparison of $50 to $5,000 was, to some degree, a contrast between apples and oranges.

My daily reading of newspaper ads also revealed another pattern. I noticed that the closer a property was to Springfield (my target area's largest town), the higher the price. Of course, that didn't discourage me, since I actually preferred an isolated spot far away from town.

The Sunday edition of the *Des Moines Register*, Iowa's largest newspaper, had the greatest number of listings of farms for sale. But most of the properties were located in other areas of the state. When a property in my area did appear, it was always for a parcel of 100 or more acres.

Since it seemed unlikely that I was going to find a property by waiting for it to appear in the classifieds, I decided to run my own advertisement. As you'll remember from Chapter One, my first ad, which specified that I wanted property with a barn or a garage on it, brought in only two responses.

I now needed to compose an ad that would generate a larger response. However, before I had a chance to write the new ad, my friend Chuck telephoned with an exciting proposition.

## Chapter Nine

# DISCOVERY BY CANOE
# AND TOPOGRAPHICAL MAP

"Hey, Ralph," Chuck said over the phone, "do you want to do some exploring? Somebody's lending me a canoe this weekend, and I thought it might be fun to paddle down the Grass River."

He didn't have to twist my arm. Ever since I had seen the river cabin in Burnt Hills I had been daydreaming about owning property on the Rock or the Grass, the two rivers which ran through my target area. Chuck, who was a hiker and a camper, had chosen the Grass because it was the more isolated of the two rivers.

Not wanting too strenuous a workout, I suggested we take two cars rather than one. That way, we wouldn't have to paddle upstream, as well as downstream.

Early on Saturday morning we drove Chuck's car and my car to a spot beside a two-lane blacktop road which crossed the Grass River on an old-fashioned steel truss bridge. We had chosen this location as the downstream point where the trip would end.

After leaving Chuck's car on the shoulder of the road, we piled into my Datsun (with the canoe on top) and headed for the river's next upstream crossing, a concrete bridge five miles to the west.

We launched the canoe under the concrete bridge and headed downstream. The river, which was about 200 feet wide at that point, wound through corn fields planted close to the water on both sides. After paddling about fifteen minutes, the flat crop land gave way to hilly, timbered ground. Occasionally, a hawk would leave its perch in one of the tall trees next to the river and circle over the water.

As we guided the canoe around a sharp bend in the river, I happened to look into the woods at a point where the land sloped sharply upwards from the river bank. Just barely visible through the trees was a cabin.

The building stood about fifty feet back from the river, thirty feet or so higher than the water. The structure, which was covered with rough, unpainted wood, looked deserted.

The cabin had been the only sign of civilization we had seen since leaving the bridge. But what was behind the cabin? I wondered whether there were any other buildings nearby, and what sort of road led to the cabin.

I was itching to beach the canoe and explore the place, but Chuck wanted to continue on down the river. As we paddled away, I kept looking back at the spot on the hill where the cabin had been visible.

*Gosh, what a wonderful place that would be to own.*

We didn't encounter any other buildings during the rest of the trip, and after tying the canoe to the top of Chuck's car, I made up my mind to return to the spot another day and approach the cabin by land.

As soon as I got home that night, I looked at a highway map. It didn't show any roads near the stretch of river between the two bridges, but that didn't mean there weren't any. Highway maps rarely show unpaved roads. What I needed was a topographical map of the area.*

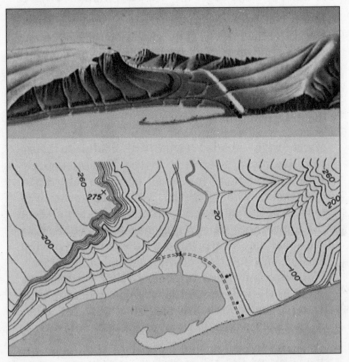

**Courtesy of U.S. Geological Survey**

* Topographical maps, with their contour lines indicating elevation, allow you to see not only the location and shape of mountains and valleys, but also the steepness of the terrain. Other features are also depicted in minute detail,

I ordered twelve of the "7.5-minute quadrangle" maps, two covering the river near the cabin, the remainder covering other areas within my target area. (The maps, which are available from the U.S. Geological Survey, cost $2.50 each.) During the next few days, while waiting for the maps to arrive, I found it hard to focus my attention on the writing project I was working on. My mind kept wandering back to thoughts of the cabin.

Maybe the building was owned by a little old lady who lived in some small town. I would knock on the door to her home and she would invite me to come in. We would sit on a sofa in the parlor and talk. She would be a widow and I would be charming, and she'd enjoy my company. When the subject of the cabin came up, she'd say that she was glad to get rid of it. I would buy it for three or four thousand dollars.

When the topo maps arrived in a long cardboard tube six days later, I unrolled them and spread them out on the floor. Although each map was about the size of a highway map, the scale of the topo maps was much larger. Whereas the whole state of Iowa is depicted on one side of a highway map, it takes 1,074 topo maps to represent the same area.

The two bridges where we started and ended the trip were clearly visible on the map, and by using a ruler I determined that the distance between the two bridges was five and a half miles as the crow flies. However, that didn't take into account the bends in the river. To measure the actual distance we paddled, I laid a piece of string over the river, then held the string up to the map's scale. We had covered eight and three-quarter miles.

I couldn't remember how many bends in the river we had gone through before coming upon the cabin, so I didn't know,

including streams, rivers, roads, railroads, cities and towns. In fact, if you use the "7.5-minute quadrangle" series of maps, which show the most detail, you'll even be able to see individual farmhouses, barns, and other works of man.

exactly, where the cabin was. However, during the trip I had looked at my watch periodically and noted what time it was when we started, when we saw the cabin, and when the trip ended.

It had taken us almost sixty minutes to reach the cabin, and another ninety minutes to complete the trip. Therefore, the cabin had been roughly two-fifths of the way down the river.

Looking at the map, I noticed a small black dot, about the size of a pin head, almost exactly two-fifths of the distance down the river. The dot, which indicated the presence of a building, was on the correct side of the river and was the only building marker between the two bridges. The contour lines around the dot also jibed with what I remembered about the terrain surrounding the building.

The map showed that a gravel road ran parallel to, and half a mile south of, the river. Most interesting, though, was the depiction of a dirt lane leading from the gravel road to the cabin.

\* \* \* \*

A few days later, after rolling the topo maps up in their cardboard tube and making sure my compass was in the car, I started out towards the river.

The maps indicated that I'd have to negotiate two forks in the gravel road before I arrived at the spot where the dirt lane veered off to the cabin. At each intersection and bend in the gravel road, I stopped the car and looked at the map. I wanted to confirm that I was where I should be, according to the map.

Although I hadn't reached the cabin yet, just following my progress on the map was exciting. Whenever I came to a farmhouse or barn, I'd stop and look at the map to locate the black dot representing that building.

After about two miles I arrived at the spot where the dirt lane should have been, but it wasn't there. I drove back and forth a mile in each direction along the gravel road looking for the dirt lane, but all I saw was pasture land.

I couldn't figure it out. Could I be at the wrong place?

About a mile down the gravel road I did find a lane which, according to the map, headed towards the river, then dead-ended.

I started down this road, which wound through timbered country and was only one lane wide. As I came around a curve, I almost ran into two people standing in the middle of the road.

One was a man about forty-five, tall and skinny and with a week's growth of beard. He wore a hunting cap and dirty work clothes. The other person was a boy about ten years old.

I stuck my head out the car window and said, "I hope this isn't a private road. I'm just exploring."

"That's ok," the man said. "Just don't steal my cows." He and the boy then walked into the woods. They were out of sight within ten seconds.

I drove on down the lane, and after a few more turns and up-and-down hills, the road ended at an opening into a corn field.

I considered getting out of the Datsun and walking through the woods to the river, and then locating the cabin, but I was apprehensive. The corn field was obviously private land, and the man and boy might be waiting in the woods to see what I did next, so I gave up.

During the drive back home I made up my mind to take another canoe trip. This time I'd go by myself and get out to explore the cabin.

\* \* \* \*

Two weeks later, after renting a canoe in Springfield and

transporting it up to the river, I shoved off from the shore at the upper bridge. This time, with only one car, I'd have to paddle back upstream on the return trip. However, since it hadn't rained for a couple of weeks, the water was now low and wasn't flowing fast.

During the paddle downstream I pictured myself owning the cabin. There would be a huge stone fireplace inside, and a comfortable sofa would be positioned right in front of the fire. I could relax by lying down on the sofa and reading books, and whenever I'd look out the window I'd see the river below.

When I arrived at the cabin I pulled the canoe up on the bank. For extra measure I tied it to a tree, since I didn't want the canoe to drift off and leave me marooned.

As I walked up the hill to the cabin, it became obvious that the place wasn't being used. There were tall weeds and grass around the building, and I didn't see any evidence that anyone had trampled or driven over the ground.

The cabin, which was about 15x25 feet in size, was one story high. It had eight windows, two doors, and a gable roof which was covered with asphalt roll roofing. Although the building looked old and unused, it appeared to be in pretty good condition.

After looking around to make sure there was nobody else there, I walked up to one of the windows and peered in. The inside of the cabin, which was all one big room, had plastered walls and ceiling. Two steel cots were stacked up in a corner, along with a number of old wooden chairs and tables.

As I looked down towards the river, which was barely visible through the trees, I imagined myself owning the property and taking canoe trips and swims whenever I wanted.

Wandering around to the back of the cabin, I noticed a dirt road which led from the cabin to the top of the hill. I walked up the road and saw that it opened into a pasture where a herd of cows were grazing.

I now realized that the road, which had originally extended through the pasture, had probably been plowed under years ago. If I bought the property and wanted to get to the cabin from the county road, I'd have to drive through someone else's pasture, and to do that the owner of the pasture would have to grant me an easement. But even if I could get an easement, it still could be difficult, or maybe even impossible, to drive across the approximately 2,000 feet of pasture during the snows of winter and the rains of spring.

During the walk back to the canoe I reluctantly accepted the fact that the lack of access to the property made the cabin impractical. Even though the building's setting was beautiful, I would have to continue my search.

The paddle back up the river was exhausting, and by the time I reached the car I had resolved to use another method of hunting for property, a method less strenuous than canoeing.

Why not, I asked myself, just drive down country roads until I found some land that looked interesting?

## CHAPTER TEN

# DRIVING THE ROADS

All I had to do, I reasoned, was drive down enough country roads and eventually I'd find properties that could be bought.

The first road I explored was gravel, heading northwest out of Springfield. I drove slowly and kept my eyes out for buildings that looked abandoned. There weren't any other vehicles on the road, and I was able to mosey along at about twenty-five miles per hour.

Most of the countryside was flat, planted with corn and soybeans. Occasionally, there were timbered areas that were too hilly for cultivation.

Just over the top of a slight hill in the road I saw a barn. The building stood in a pasture about 100 feet back from the road. There were a few large trees nearby, but no other buildings. A large "Keep Out" sign was nailed to a board in the fence that ran by the side of the road.

The barn, which had a hip roof and was two stories high, was covered with wood siding. The building's big doors, wide enough to drive a farm wagon through, had fallen off and were lying on the ground, just barely visible under the tall grass. Part of the building's metal roof had been bent up, as if the wind had caught it.

*I could repair it. Maybe even build an apartment on the second floor, with a big window and a view of the pasture and trees.*

I decided to inquire about the place at one of the neighbors. I drove south down the road, and after about a quarter mile came to a farmhouse. There were hogs in a pen next to a barn, and a car in the driveway. No one answered the door, though, when I knocked. I didn't have any better luck at a mobile home north of the deserted barn.

However, I knew that I could find out who owned property by inquiring at the courthouse. On the trip back to town, I used the Datsun's odometer to measure the distance. It was 7.3 miles from the barn to the center of town.

At the tax assessor's office in the Columbia County courthouse I was shown a number of large aerial photographs of that part of the county. Using the scale on the photograph, along with the mileage reading, the assessor and I were able to locate the property. In fact, the barn itself was actually visible on the photograph.

After leafing through a file cabinet, the assessor gave me the name and address of the property's owner, a Mr. Robert

Cunningham. He lived on State Street in Cedar Rapids, a city about 110 miles north of Springfield.

The courthouse records didn't contain the owner's telephone number, so I walked over to the public library, where I found a phone book for Cedar Rapids. However, there was no Robert Cunningham, or any Cunninghams, listed on State St. When I returned home, I called the directory assistance operator, but she also had no listing.

Later that day I mailed the following note:

> Dear Mr. Cunningham: I am interested in buying a small acreage with an old barn on it, and while driving around the county I noticed your barn in Lehigh Township. (I checked the ownership records at the county courthouse.)
>
> Is there any chance you would like to talk to me about selling a small amount of your land and the barn?
>
> My telephone number is 319–555–2293, but I've also included a stamped envelope, in case you'd rather contact me by mail.      Sincerely, Ralph Turner

Mr. Cunningham telephoned me five days later. "I can't sell off any frontage on the gravel road," he said, "because that would restrict access to the rear pasture. But I'd be willing to sell 100 acres if I got the right price."

I told him I could afford only ten or twenty acres, and thanked him for calling. After hanging up, I was discouraged. It didn't seem very likely that I'd stumble upon my dream property by merely driving through the country. Maybe I would have to be more creative in my search efforts.

In addition to driving, how about if I started talking to people?

CHAPTER ELEVEN

# MISCELLANEOUS
# SEARCH METHODS

I now added a new activity to my rural explorations. Whenever I came upon a farmer near the road, I'd stop to see if he knew of any land for sale. If he didn't, I'd ask if he could think of anyone else I should talk to. The farmers were invariably friendly, but on those occasions when I was given leads on properties, the parcels were always too large.

Then I began to wonder, why rely on chance encounters? Maybe there was a way of meeting lots of farmers at one place. The first thing that came to mind was rural auctions.

From then on whenever I attended an auction, I made a point of talking to as many people as possible. Because I felt uncomfortable just walking up to a stranger at an auction and saying, "Hi, I'm looking for some land to buy," I relied on a less direct approach.

After asking one of the people standing next to me a question about whatever item was up for sale at the moment, I could easily start up a conversation. Usually we talked about the weather, this year's crop, or the state of the economy. Eventually the person might ask, "You from around here?" At that point I could easily answer, "No, but I'm looking for land to buy in this area."

Another idea I tried was posters. Using a felt marking pen, I created a poster announcing, "Land Wanted." I included my telephone number, as well as a brief description of the type of property I wanted.

# LAND WANTED

WANTED TO BUY: 10 TO 40 RURAL ACRES, SOME OR ALL TIMBER, ON DIRT OR GRAVEL ROAD, IN FILLMORE, BLAIR, OR COLUMBIA COUNTY.
319 - 555 - 2293

After making about twenty-five photocopies of the poster, I tacked them up at gas stations, coffee shops, and hardware stores in a number of small rural communities. Two people called me as a result of seeing the poster, but both properties were out of my price range.

I considered slipping copies of the notice under the windshield wipers of vehicles parked along the road at country auctions, but I discarded that idea as inappropriate. Mass-leafleting might be acceptable in big-city parking lots, but it seemed too pushy for rural sensibilities.

If I had been willing to move away from Springfield, I might have considered renting a piece of rural property and moving to the country. As a rural resident, it would be easier to learn about land that could be purchased. I'd also be able to get a feel for the area to see if I'd like living there.

I also considered attending rural churches. During the socializing that usually occurs after the service, there would be a chance to tell lots of people that I was looking for land to buy in the area. Since members of small churches are always interested in adding new people to their congregations, I figured this would be one of the best ways of developing new leads.

However, since I hadn't gone to church regularly since high school, it seemed dishonest to attend church merely to find land. If I *did* buy property as a result of attending church, I'd then feel uncomfortable *not* attending services.

I came up with other ideas, though. One Saturday, rather than having my hair cut in Springfield, I drove down to a barbershop in one of the small towns south of here. The haircut cost two dollars less than what I normally pay, and I made a point of telling the barber about my land search.

I also stopped in and talked to the loan officers at a number of rural banks. I asked if they had foreclosed on any farms which they now wanted to get rid of. One bank did have two such properties, but both of them were large acreages with substantial farmhouses.

I tried to think of people who had lots of contact with rural land owners and who, as a result, might know about owners interested in selling land. Sheriff's deputies, township supervisors, attorneys, and land surveyors came to mind, and my plan was to contact some of those people after I had run another newspaper advertisement. (I had already gone to the courthouses in a number of counties and asked the tax assessors if they knew of any land for sale. I picked up a number of good leads, but nothing panned out.)

I even considered offering a finder's fee. This tactic had worked perfectly years ago when I was attending college in San Francisco. I had asked all my friends if they knew of any place where I could live free, in exchange for work. No one did, so I decided to offer a $25 reward for information about such a live-in situation.

Two days later I got a call from one of the friends who had previously claimed he knew of nothing. Now, he said, he remembered that a doctor friend of his had been looking for someone to do janitorial work. I applied for the job and got it, then spent the next two years living, rent free, in the basement of a medical clinic in exchange for ten hours per week of vacuuming and floor washing.

So now, in Iowa, I considered creating a poster offering a $100 reward for information about small properties for sale. The poster would have to be worded carefully so that I would be obligated to pay the reward only if I bought a property.

I never got beyond composing a rough draft of the poster. By that time I was being swamped, as you'll see in the next chapter, with responses to my second newspaper advertisement.

## CHAPTER TWELVE

# MY SECOND NEWSPAPER ADVERTISEMENT

*Chuck:* I don't understand, Ralph, why you're holding out for a piece of property with a barn on it.

*Me:* Some day I'm going to buy a tractor, and I don't want to store it out in the rain.

*Chuck:* But by looking only at properties with barns, the search becomes that much harder. You're restricting yourself, and probably overlooking a number of good bargains. A barn can always be built after you buy a property.

Maybe Chuck was right. I went home and wrote another ad:

| | | |
|---|---|---|
| ~me will ). Extras ,ators and -555-8261 est drive. | number on answering machine. Will get back to you. | ɔɔɔ-0202. |
| | WANTED TO BUY: Three to thirty acres (some or all timber) within 25 miles of Springfield. 555-2293. | WANT TO E lame, crippl hogs, sows, i all kinds of cattle, goats ponies, will |
| TRAILER - ng. rear microwave ~~ndition. | FOR SALE - 90 acres, 71 acres tillable, located in D Maines Township Tyler | Licensed. registered w. before you |

The ad which I had run a couple of months earlier had brought only two responses, so I decided to place this new ad in three different small-town newspapers at the same time. I got over thirty responses.

The first caller had forty acres of timber for sale. When I asked about the type of road it was on, he said the only way to get to the property was over a county-owned dirt road.

"I don't think I want property on a dirt road," I said. "I need a place I can get to all year round, even during the spring rains."

"When it's too muddy to get through", he said, "well hell, you shouldn't be going there! Ha Ha Ha."

The second caller had twenty acres over in Blair County.

*Me:* Is there an access road onto the property?

*Seller:* I put in a driveway, but it's on the parcel to the west of mine.

*Me:* I don't understand.

*Seller:* Before I bought it, I was under the impression... I mean, they showed me where the boundaries were. After I bought it, I laid a culvert in the ditch next to the county road and had gravel brought in for a driveway. Then the neighbor – he farms to the west – came over and said I had put the driveway on his property, not on mine.

*Me:* By mistake?

*Seller:* Yes. I was just going by what I was told.*

I took a look at the parcel, but it was so flat as to be boring. The owner's experience, however, made me realize that I shouldn't accept as fact everything said by a seller or his agent.

---

* The matter is now being litigated.

Another fellow put a message on my answering machine saying he had a 14-acre farm for sale. He left his name and the name of the small town where he lived. But, he said, he didn't have a phone.

I drove to the town the next day. At the town's only business, a tiny grocery store, I mentioned the man's name to the lady behind the counter, and said that he didn't have a phone. "Oh," she said, "he's one of them Amish." Then she gave me directions to his farm.

The property was on the outskirts of town, and as I pulled into the driveway next to the farmhouse, I noticed that there weren't any cars, trucks, or tractors in sight. There were, however, two black buggies parked next to the barn. A young man, in his twenties and with a long beard, came out from the barn. He had on a straw hat, and his shirt and trousers, which were clean and almost new, looked hand-made.

He had used the pay phone in town, he said, to leave his message. He showed me the property, but it included the barn and a house, and was on a heavily travelled road.

I stayed around for over a half hour, though, talking about the carpentry projects he was working on. He was soft spoken and shy. I had never talked to an Amish person before, and he intrigued me.

The next call was from a farmer who had seventeen acres of pasture that he wanted $750 per acre for. The $12,750 asking price was more than I could spend, but when he described the large oak trees on the property, I decided to take a look at it.

The next day was a cold, snowy February morning, and after driving down to the man's farm, he insisted that, before we look at the pasture, I come in and warm up. In the kitchen, his wife served me coffee and home-made cookies.

The 17-acre parcel consisted mainly of open ground, but on

one-quarter of the property, at the back of the parcel and away from the road, was the grove of oak trees. Most of the trees were huge, some almost three feet in diameter. It would make a beautiful building spot.

A deep gully, about five feet wide and three feet deep, crossed from one side of the property to the other. The gully was eroded badly, and didn't look like a natural watercourse.

> *Me:* Where does the stream come from?
>
> *Farmer:* That's drainage from my fields. I laid drainage tile two years ago. When the seventeen acres is sold, I'll want an easement.
>
> *Me:* I don't understand.
>
> *Farmer:* I have to drain my fields when they get wet. After the pasture's sold, I don't want nobody blocking off that ditch. But don't worry, easements like that, they're common. It's done all the time.

Maybe so, I thought, but I didn't like the idea of granting to a neighbor (and any future owners of the neighbor's land) the right to divert unlimited quantities of agricultural run-off onto my property. I decided to keep my eye out for such ditches when I visited other parcels.

Another caller, an elderly lady who lived back East most of the year, said she had twenty wooded acres for sale. The parcel, she told me over the phone, was on a cliff overlooking the Rock River.

> *Me:* What kind of road is the property on?
>
> *Lady:* County gravel. You go through the Lang– worthy farm to get to it.
>
> *Me:* The property doesn't abut the county

road?

*Lady:* Oh, no. It's very secluded.

*Me:* How far onto the Langworthy farm do you have to go?

*Lady:* About half a mile, maybe.

*Me:* Has an easement been recorded that permits you to cross over the Langworthy property?

*Lady:* That's a good question. I don't know. We have access rights, though, if that's what you mean.

*Me:* How much are you asking?

*Lady:* Well, the thing is... I really don't know whether I want to sell. Maybe I'll retire there and build on it. So I'm not going to say, 'I want such and such for it.' If you're interested, make an offer.

I drove down and met the lady, and we looked at the property together. It was beautiful. But there was no road, not even a path, from the county road to the property. We had to follow a circuitous route around the edge of three corn fields to get to the place. The expense of connecting electricity or rural water would be exorbitant.

* * * *

Many of the people who responded to my ad wanted to sell large acreages. Even though my ad had specified three to thirty acres, I received eight calls from owners with more than fifty acres to sell, and four of those calls were for parcels 115 acres or larger.

Sometimes I'd get so excited when someone called that I'd

forget what questions to ask. Only after hanging up would I realize that I hadn't gotten enough information. After this happened a few times, I decided to get organized. I wrote out on a piece of paper a list of questions to ask each caller:

1. How many acres?
2. Where is it located? (including township and section)
3. What type of land? (crop, timber, pasture; hilly, flat)
4. Any buildings? (house, barn)
5. Is there water? (well, pond, rural water)
6. What type of road is it on? (paved, gravel, dirt)
7. Utilities hooked up? (electricity, telephone, rural water, septic system)
8. What are the taxes?
9. How long have you owned it?
10. Why are you selling?
11. Is there a deed to this specific parcel, or are you selling off a piece from a larger tract?
12. Do you own it outright, or is there a mortgage or contract outstanding?
13. Is there an access road leading from the county road onto your property?
14. Are the boundaries marked by fences?
15. What is the asking price?
16. How do I get to the property? (directions)

As I was to find out from the next caller, even when the right questions were asked, simple answers weren't always forth-coming.

## Chapter Thirteen

# CLEAR TITLE

*Me:* Do you own the property free and clear?

*Seller:* Yup.... sort of.

The seller, a man in his sixties, had telephoned me in response to my latest newspaper ad. He had ten acres of timber that he wanted $11,000 for. The property was on a gravel road about thirty-five miles northeast of Springfield, in Tyler County.

Although $11,000 was more than I wanted to spend, a number of improvements had been made to the property, and I felt I should at least take a look at it. When the seller bought the property nine years earlier, he had cut down some trees and brought in a mobile home. Electrical and rural water hookups were added, a septic system was installed, and a road was graded to the mobile home.

When he met me at the property to show me around, I was immediately enthralled with the setting. The mobile home had been removed, and the view from the clearing was beautiful. The property, which was quite hilly, looked out over the rolling pastures of the surrounding farms. The closest neighbor was more than a mile away, and as we stood in the sunlight that warm fall morning, the only sounds I heard were the wind blowing through the trees and the squirrels rummaging through leaves on the ground.

I had asked if he owned the property free and clear because I wondered whether a lender held a mortgage.

*Me:* What do you mean, you own the property "sort of?"

*Seller:* I sold it to Kyle. That'd be my son. He'll give you a quit claim deed, but you pay me. I really own it.

*Me:* Have you talked to an attorney about this?

*Seller:* Yup, but he thinks Kyle and me have to run through some legal rigmarole. It'll take forty days if we do it his way. The attorney's just trying to make more money, that's for sure. A quit claim from Kyle to you is all it needs, if you ask me.

I wasn't going to accept a quit claim deed, but I didn't want to antagonize him by admitting it, at least not at this early stage, so I changed the subject to the property's boundary lines. During our walk through the woods I had noticed that only three sides of the parcel were fenced.

*Me:* Where is the western boundary?

*Seller:* The other side of that dirt road. At least that's what *I* figure.

*Me:* What do you mean?

*Seller:* Cedric says the road's on his land.

*Me:* Who's Cedric?

*Seller:* The guy who bought the property.

*Me:* Didn't your son buy it?

A slight scowl appeared on the man's face, and I got the impression he thought I was stupid.

*Seller:* My son *did* buy it.

*Me:* I'm confused.

*Seller:* My son bought, then Cedric bought.

*Me:* Then isn't Cedric the person I'd buy it from?

*Seller:* Course not! Cedric don't own *this* property. His is the *west* ten.

*Me:* How's that?

*Seller:* Kyle sold the west ten to Cedric. You'd buy the east ten.

I wasn't sure I understood, but I decided to drop the subject for the time being.

*Me:* When your son sold to Cedric, was the property surveyed?

*Seller:* Nope.

*Me:* Was it surveyed when you bought it?

Seller: Nope. No need to.

We resumed our walk through the woods. Most of the trees were deciduous, but here and there were some evergreens. The trunks of some of the trees were two feet in diameter.

At the clearing where the mobile home had sat, there were a number of old cars. A red sedan, a relic from the 1950s, rested on cinder blocks, its wheels removed. Doors were missing from some of the cars, and a rusting sedan, its hood open and mangled, had no engine.

*Me:* Who owns the cars?

*Seller:* Smith.

*Me:* Who's he?

*Seller:* Tenant.

*Me:* Is he still renting?

*Seller:* Well, they wasn't *exactly* renting, him and his wife. They bought, sort of.

Me: They *bought* the property?

*Seller:* Kyle paid for that contract to be drew up, but he never got a plugged nickel the whole time they was here. Talk to Mr. Calhoun, he'll tell you.

I was almost afraid to ask, but I had to.

*Me:* Mr. Calhoun? Who's he?

*Seller:* Attorney. But I still say we don't need no attorney. Just a quit claim deed. Them cars, now I'm not supposed to move 'em. They'll sue me quick as lightning if I so much as lay a finger on 'em.

On the other side of the clearing in a grove of short pine trees, two birds were perched on tree limbs, chattering to each other.

*Me:* I like the place, but I'm concerned about getting clear title, considering the number of transfers to different people. I'd like to talk to the attorney. Then I'll get back to you.

*Seller:* Whatever. But I should tell you, the wife's

got a friend, a real estate agent, and we might just have her start showing the property. That'd mean a commission. Extra.

*Me:* I'd also like to return to the property on my own and take another look. Is that ok?

*Seller:* No matter to me, but I don't know what you think you're gonna find.

During the drive back to Springfield, I used my car's odometer to measure the exact distance to my home. Although it was only thirty-eight miles, the roads weren't the type that could be negotiated at a steady fifty-five miles per hour. Much of the drive was over gravel, and there were a lot of "T" intersections, stop signs, and sharp, right-angle turns. The trip took fifty-two minutes.

The next morning I called Mr. Calhoun, the attorney.

*Attorney:* Oh, yes, the old man's had quite a time with that property. He sold twenty acres to his son on an interest-free contract, but the son never made any payments. The son then sold off the ten acres on the west.

*Me:* Is that the property Cedric owns?

*Attorney:* Yes. Then the son sold the east ten acres. That's the property you're interested in. That sale was an interest-free contract, too, but there was a disagreement between the buyers and the son, and the buyers never paid anything on the contract. Eventually, the buyers deeded back their interest to the son, but they never removed the old cars.

*Me:* Who would I buy the property from?

*Attorney:* The father.

    *Me:* He wants me to accept a quit claim from the son.

*Attorney:* No, the father should cause the contract to be forfeited.

    *Me:* How long would that take?

*Attorney:* The son will have to be given thirty days notice, but I'm not even sure the sheriff can find him. Service might have to be by publication. The whole process will probably take about six weeks.

I returned to the property a few days later. I wanted to explore the place by myself, without the seller following me around. I was curious to find out what condition the fence was in, and to see what the rest of the land looked like.

This time it was an overcast, foggy day, but the property seemed even prettier than before. When I looked into the woods, the mist in the air made the distant trees appear blurry, almost soft.

The ground was hilly, and after climbing up and down a number of gullies, I was winded. Sitting down to rest on a tree that had fallen to the ground, I tried to imagine what it would be like to own the property.

*Even though it's hilly, I bet I could get a tractor in here. I could pull these dead trees out, then cut them for firewood. Gosh, I like this place.*

I sat still and listened.

Listening to the sounds of nature is something I love to do. I can still remember the first time I did it, although that was thirty-seven years ago. I was fourteen years old, and my friend Tommy and I and his father were riding in their 1956 Ford station wagon through the country. Tommy's father was at the wheel, and we were on our way to their summer home in the mountains.

At a spot where the road wound through the woods, Tommy's father slowed down and pulled the car to the side of the pavement. Shutting off the engine, he said, "OK, boys, out of the car. Come with me."

He walked off into the woods, Tommy and I following. There was no trail. Tommy's father just bushwhacked his way through the trees and shrubs. When we were about 400 feet into the woods, he said, "OK, boys. Sit down. Close your eyes, then listen."

All three of us sat down on the ground. Although it was a sunny morning, the tree cover was so thick that it seemed like dusk. Tommy said, "Listen to what, Dad?" His father answered in a soft voice, "Listen to the quiet."

Tommy and I exchanged glances, and I held back a laugh. Then I closed my eyes. At first, I didn't hear anything. After a few moments, though, I heard a bird whistle. A few seconds later another bird, in a different location, responded with the same whistle.

We sat on the ground for about five minutes, just listening. Then Tommy's father stood up, motioned us to follow, and we returned to the car. In the years since then, I've always enjoyed sitting down in the wilderness and listening to whatever there is to hear.

Now, as I rested on the log on the 10-acre parcel, I heard the wind in the trees. There was also the distant sound of a farm tractor, its muffled roar just barely audible. Somebody was probably plowing in a field a mile or so away.

After a few minutes I resumed my hike. I walked the entire perimeter of the property. The fence, which was constructed of wood posts and three strands of barbed wire, was in pretty good condition.

Next, I looked at the clearing where the mobile home had sat. The ground had been churned up, possibly when the trailer had been pulled out. I looked for the water and septic pipes, but couldn't find them.

*I wonder how I'd locate those. It might take a heck of a lot of digging to uncover them.*

It was getting dark, and I needed to return to Springfield. But there was one more thing to do. I wanted to talk to the closest neighbor. He might know something about the property.

\* \* \* \*

A little more than a mile down the road stood a single-story, wood frame house. A John Deere tractor sat in the driveway, and behind the house was a large red barn.

I knocked on the door of the farmhouse, but no one answered. As I walked around toward the barn, I saw a young man working on a piece of machinery.

> *Me:* Hi. I was looking at that 10-acre parcel that's for sale down the road on the north side. There used to be a trailer there. Do you know anything about the property?

> *Farmer:* What you going to use the place for?

> *Me:* Oh, I want a few acres where I can get away on the weekends. Just a place with some trees.

> *Farmer:* Where you from?

> *Me:* Springfield.

> *Farmer:* What's he asking for that place?

> *Me:* $11,000.

66

*Farmer:* Too much. Shucks, that ground ain't worth nothing. Mind you, I ain't trying to talk you out of buying it.

*Me:* But he's put utilities in, water, septic and electric. That's worth quite a lot.

*Farmer:* Maybe. But if all you want's some timber... Shoot, you can buy timber for a lot less than $1,100 an acre.

*Me:* A 10-acre parcel?

*Farmer:* Maybe. Like I said, I ain't trying to talk you out of it. I just don't think it's worth it. Now, if you're looking for timber, you should talk to Clide, over by the church. He might be wanting to sell his parent's old place.

*Me:* How many acres is that?

*Farmer:* Eighty, I think.

*Me:* That's way more than I can afford.

*Farmer:* All I know, them ten acres ain't worth what he's asking. But I ain't trying to talk you out of it.

We talked for a few more minutes, mainly about tractors. He asked who I was, and we exchanged names. He had a peculiar last name, one that was easy to remember. I didn't realize it then, but I'd learn more about him a few weeks later.

During the drive back home, I weighed the property's good and bad features.

*There's no question the place is beautiful. If I built a cabin, I'd already have water and electricity. I get such a nice feeling when I'm there. And although $11,000 is more than I want to spend, maybe the seller will accept less. The main problem is its location.*

*Fifty-two minutes is a long drive. That's almost two hours each time I want to visit the property.*

A few days later at the Tyler County courthouse, the tax assessor showed me an aerial photograph of the appropriate section of the county. Each owner's parcel was outlined by a felt pen, and each parcel had its soil quality indicated by code.

*Assessor:* The soil on the parcel you're interested in isn't particularly good, so from an agricultural standpoint the property isn't worth much. That 10-acre parcel is assessed at $1,295. But that doesn't mean the property is worth only that. Assessed value is below market value.

*Me:* If I bought that place, would it need to be surveyed?

*Assessor:* No, not as far as we're concerned. But whether you should have it surveyed to protect yourself, that's a different matter.

*Me:* Can I find out how much the taxes are?

*Assessor:* Sure. Let me see.... here it is. They're $18.00 a year, and they're paid up.

*Me:* Is it possible to find out how much the owner paid for the 20-acre parcel when he bought it?

*Assessor:* Maybe. But you'll have to go to the Recorder's Office. They can look at the deed.

Before I left her office, the assessor gave me the number of the book and the page number where the deed was recorded. Down the hall at the Recorder's Office the clerk used the book and page number to find the deed, which had been recorded in 1983.

Although the price that the present owner paid wasn't specifically noted on the deed, there was, the clerk said, a way of calculating what the price had been.

Whenever a purchaser buys a piece of property, he pays a transfer tax to the county. If you know how much tax was paid on a transaction, you can determine the selling price by referring to the Real Estate Transfer Tax Table.

The deed for the larger 20-acre parcel indicated that $2.75 in tax had been collected. After referring to the table, the clerk said that the present owner had paid between $2,501 and $3,000 for the parcel.

*　*　*　*

I thought a lot about the property over the next few days. It was the nicest piece of land I had found, but the asking price was way over my budget.

Then one night after going to bed early, I happened to wake up at three in the morning. I couldn't get back to sleep, and after thinking about the property for awhile, I decided to drive up there and visit it right then. It would be fun to see the place in the dark.

When I arrived at the property and got out of my car, the first thing I noticed was how light the sky was. The moon was out, and I was surprised at how much of the ground and the trees I could see.

I started walking up the dirt road that followed the property's western boundary. I had brought a flashlight with me, but the moon was bright enough that I could keep to the road without using it.

At the back of the property, the dirt road opened onto a clearing. I lay down on the ground on my back. The air was cold, but I had a heavy coat and gloves on. The stars were shining above me, framed by the treetops at the edge of the clearing.

*Gosh, this place feels so peaceful, I'd almost like to fall asleep right here.*

The next day I told Chuck about the property.

*Me:* I checked at the courthouse and discovered that the seller paid only about $3,000 when he bought the twenty acres, nine years ago. But now he's wanting $11,000 for just ten of those acres. Fifteen hundred to $11,000 seems like a huge appreciation, even considering the improvements. Maybe he'll accept a low-ball offer.

*Chuck:* He may or may not accept a low offer, but don't be swayed by what somebody *paid* for property. It wouldn't matter if he paid only $75 for it. That's not the point. The only valid question is, how much is the property worth *today*. In other words, how much are similar properties going for today.

\* \* \* \*

During the next couple of weeks I visited the property four more times. It seemed as if I liked the place more each time I saw it. But there was something inside me that was holding me back from immediately making an offer. I had doubts, but I wasn't sure why I had them. Maybe I should continue looking for other properties, I thought.

Remembering my conversation with the farmer down the road who had the peculiar name, I decided to follow up on his tip about Clide's eighty acres over by the church. Maybe I could buy off a small portion of his parcel. However, I didn't know Clide's last name, so I'd have to talk to the farmer again.

Looking through the phone book, I found only one listing for that peculiar name. I dialed the number, and the phone at the other end was picked up after the twelfth ring.

>*Me:* My name's Ralph Turner. I think I talked to you a few weeks ago about that 10-acre parcel down the road from you.
>
>*Man:* Nope, you never talked to me.
>
>*Me:* Oh, sorry. It was somebody with the same last name.
>
>*Man:* That's my cousin. He's been trying to buy that parcel for more than two years. Made a reasonable offer on it, but the owner won't budge.

So that was it! The farmer had kept telling me how he wasn't trying to talk me out of buying the property, but he had repeated the reassurance so many times that something seemed strange. He had wanted it for himself!

We chatted for a few minutes and he gave me Clide's telephone number. I called Clide a few days later, but he didn't want to break up the 80-acre parcel.

* * * *

I decided to talk to Chuck again.

>*Me:* I can't decide whether to make an offer on that 10-acre parcel. Although it's the most beautiful place I've seen, it's got a few drawbacks.
>
>*Chuck:* You'll never find the perfect place.
>
>*Me:* I realize that, but something inside me is

71

holding me back.

*Chuck:* Sometimes you've just got to act. If you don't, you'll be just like the minister in that old joke about the flood.

*Me:* What joke is that?

*Chuck:* Haven't you heard that? The river is flooding, and the water's so high it's flooded the first floor of the minister's house. He climbs onto the roof, and somebody paddles by in a boat and says, "Jump in the boat, I'll save you." The minister responds, "You go on. God will save me." An hour later, the water has risen to the roof, and the minister's up on the chimney. A sheriff's helicopter arrives, and the pilot yells down, "Grab the rope, I'll save you." The minister responds, "You go on. God will save me." Half an hour later, the water rises above the chimney, and the minister drowns. In heaven, he asks God, "Why didn't you save me?" God replies, "You crazy fool, I sent you a boat and a helicopter. What more did you want?" So Ralph, if this 10-acre parcel is as nice as you say, maybe it's the property that God has sent you.

I agonized over the problem for the next two days. Although the property was beautiful, I worried that it was too far away. Since I couldn't make up my mind, I decided to make a low offer on the property. If the offer wasn't accepted, I'd forget it and continue my search.

I called the seller on the phone. "The property," I said, "isn't exactly what I'm looking for, but I'd like to make you an offer of $8,000."

He answered immediately, without hesitation. "I won't accept anything less than $11,000."

As I hung up the phone, I felt relieved, but also worried. Relieved that I wasn't buying a property that was too far away, but worried that I'd never find such a pretty place again.

I needn't have worried. In a few days I would be shown a map which would make finding small properties a lot easier.

CHAPTER FOURTEEN

# ROAD NOISE AND PLAT MAPS

"Don't build a house on a paved road," the elderly man said. "We did, and we wished we hadn't."

He had been fixing a fence by the side of the country road, and I had stopped to ask if he knew of any small properties for sale. He didn't, but we got talking about road noise. The ranch-style house that he and his wife had built after he retired sat back about 300 feet from the two-lane blacktop. The house was ten miles from the nearest town, and there weren't any close neighbors.

"Cars whiz by here doing sixty or seventy," he said. "Noise never bothered us in the city, but we moved out to the country expecting to enjoy the sound of the wind and the chirping of birds. Ha! When we're in the living room or in bed, we hear every darn fool that drives by."

After starting off in my car again, I turned onto the first gravel road I came to. It was a pleasant surprise. Unlike so many of the roads in Iowa, which are as straight as a row of corn, this road led through hilly countryside, winding its way back and forth among the hills.

Although I had never been on the road before, I knew from looking at a highway map that it followed the contours of the Rock River. I couldn't see the river, though, because there was a ridge of hills between the water and the road. The area was so sparsely populated that I drove for almost three miles without coming across a single house.

As I rounded one of the curves, I saw a barn. The structure was set back from the road about 200 feet, on the river side of the road. There weren't any other buildings, although I spotted an old stone foundation where there had apparently been a farmhouse. Behind the barn, the hills rose at least seventy feet. There were some trees on the hills, but not enough to be called a forest.

The barn was one and a half stories high and was in bad condition. Some of the siding was gone, and the structure's big doors were missing. Through the open doors I could see what looked like a piece of machinery, but the interior of the building was too dark to determine whether it was a tractor.

That night after returning home, I unrolled my topographical maps and spread them out on the living room floor. It took a few minutes to locate the map containing the area that I had explored. Since I'm near-sighted, I had to crouch down on my hands and knees and take my glasses off in order to see the small details of the map.

I got excited when I saw two black dots on the map representing the barn and the now-nonexistent house. A notation in the lower right-hand corner of the map indicated that the U. S. Geological Survey had created the map in 1965. Thus, the farmhouse had apparently come down sometime between 1965 and 1992. The map also showed that the river was very close to the barn, only about 600 feet away, just on the other side of the hill.

*What a great piece of land. I could build a cabin on the bank of the river, and if the machine inside the barn is a tractor, maybe it could be bought along with the land.*

To find out about the machine, I decided to buy a pair of binoculars. I had never owned a pair before. After visiting a few stores and reading a *Consumer's Reports* article on binoculars, I purchased an inexpensive pair of 7x35 Bushnell binoculars that were on sale for $21.95 at a discount store.*

I returned a few days later to the barn, which was about twenty miles from Springfield. With the binoculars, I could see that the piece of machinery was only a corn picker. But the property still fascinated me. If I built a cabin on the river, it wouldn't be visible from the road because of the hill. The site would be perfectly secluded.

To find out who owned the property, I visited the Fillmore County courthouse in Warrensburg. At the tax assessor's office, the clerk told me that the property was owned by a Clyde Peters. "He works at the bank," she said.

The simplest thing would have been to call him on the phone, but I figured he might be more willing to sell if he saw me in person. After walking over to the bank and being ushered into Mr. Peters' office, I told him I was looking for a small piece of property to buy, and that I had seen his barn.

"I've always wanted to build a house up on that hill overlooking the river," he said, "and I still might do it. I want to hold onto it. But I've got another piece of property I would be willing to sell, a 20-acre parcel down near Red Rock."

He pulled a pamphlet from his desk drawer, and turning to one of the inner pages, pointed out the property. The pamphlet consisted of page after page of specialized maps of a kind I had never seen before.

"What type of map is that?" I asked.

"It's a plat book," he said. "If you're looking for property, you

---

* The "7" in the 7x35 designation means that the observed object becomes seven times larger than when seen with the naked eye. For instance, if I use the binoculars to view a tractor that's 175 feet in front of me, it will appear to be only 25 feet away. The "35" represents the diameter of the front lens in millimeters. The larger the diameter, the brighter the image will appear, especially at night.

ought to have one. You can buy them at the courthouse." After asking him some questions about the parcel he wanted to sell, I realized that I wasn't interested in it. It was all crop land, and was too far away from Springfield.

However, the discovery of the plat book was exciting. I returned to the assessor's office to buy one, but they had sold their last copy. I eventually found one at an insurance company. It cost $19.95.

A plat map shows who owns what property. The outlines of all the farms are depicted, the sizes of all parcels noted, and the owners and their addresses are listed.

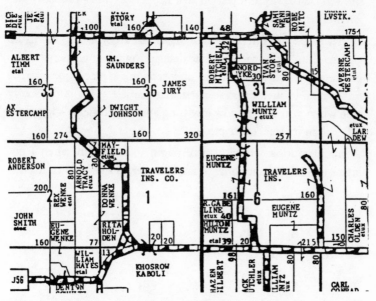

Permission granted by Farm & Home Publishers, Ltd., Belmond, Iowa

For instance, the plat map showed that Mr. Peter's barn was on an 80-acre rectangular plot. The map also showed the sizes and shapes of all the surrounding properties.

In the coming months, I came to really appreciate the value of the plat book. Not only did it show me where small parcels of property were located, it allowed me to make fewer trips to the courthouse to determine who owned specific pieces of property.

The plat book that I bought, which was 8½x11 inches in size and fifty-five pages long, actually contained both a plat book and a directory. The directory listed the rural residents of the county.

By looking at both the plat maps and the directory, I could find out not only who owned a piece of property, but who lived on it. For instance, one of the plats indicated that a particular 120-acre parcel was owned by a V. Smith, whereas the directory showed that B. Jones lived on that property. Jones probably was a renter or a relative.

Plat maps and directories are organized according to township and section.* Since the legal description of a property often makes reference to township and section, a plat book can be indispensable in locating a particular parcel. This is especially true when you don't know anything about a property's location, other than its legal description.

My plat book would also turn out to be useful when I got interested in land auctions. That, however, is a chapter in itself.

* Townships and sections are discussed on page 138.

CHAPTER FIFTEEN

# LAND AUCTIONS

Years ago I saw on television the auctioning off of a collection of expensive art objects and furniture at Sotheby's in New York City. The auctioneer, dressed in a tuxedo, spoke impeccable English and conducted the sale in a pompous manner.

In contrast with this, auctions in rural America are informal affairs. At one land auction I attended south of Springfield, a 240-acre farm was being sold. About twenty-five people, all men, were congregating around the auctioneer's truck next to the barn.

The bidding started at $300 an acre. Four men bid against each other and the price rose quickly at ten dollar increments. By the time the price got to $500, only two men were still bidding. The pace of the sale then slowed down as each man hesitated, sometimes for a minute or two, before raising the price ten dollars more. In between the bids, the auctioneer, in a loud, booming voice, maintained his non-stop spiel.

Eventually, one of the men, a short fellow with a beard who looked as if he were in his seventies, offered $590. The other bidder, who wore a John Deere cap and who looked about fifty years old, shook his head, as if to say, "I'm out." At this point, I expected the auctioneer to wrap up the sale by saying, "Going once, going twice, sold for $590 an acre."

Instead, he stopped his spiel, took a long pause, then said, "Boys, you know the property's worth more than $590 an acre.

Why don't we take a break?"

He then climbed down from the camper of his truck, where he had been standing, and walked over to the man with the John Deere cap. The auctioneer, who was obviously familiar with the bidder, put his arm around the man's shoulder. I was standing only three feet away, and I heard what was said.

The auctioneer spoke in a soft voice. "Herman," he said, "you're not going to let this property get away from you, are you? I know you've been looking for extra land. What's ten dollars more per acre? Are you going to let it slip by for just $10 more? That's only $2,400."

The bidder didn't say anything. Then the auctioneer climbed up into the camper and, resuming his booming voice, continued. "OK, boys, we had a bid of $590 per acre. Who'll give me $600." His spiel continued.

After about half a minute Herman nodded his head once. "Six hundred," yelled the auctioneer. "I've got six hundred. Who'll give me $610?"

Nobody raised the bid, but everyone's eyes were now on the bearded man. After about two minutes of patter the auctioneer said, "Let's take another break, boys."

This time, after climbing down from the camper, he went over to the bearded man. The auctioneer didn't put his arm around this fellow, but he got close to him and spoke to him real quietly for about three minutes. Then the auctioneer returned to the camper and started the auction again.

"I've got $600, who'll give me $610?" A minute went by, during which nobody bid. Then the bearded man wiggled his finger, raising the price to $610.

"I've got $610," said the auctioneer. "Who'll give me $620?" He kept up his spiel for a few more minutes, but didn't call any more time-outs. The property sold for $610 per acre.

\* \* \* \*

I attended a number of auctions of rural property, and in each case my plat book came in handy. When a land sale was advertised in the newspaper, the township and section where the property was located were always mentioned in the ad. By referring to my plat map, I was able to see the shape of the parcel, and then to locate the property on a topographical map. This allowed me to get an idea of what the land was like without having to go out and visit it.

Small properties without a farmhouse, however, were very rarely sold at auction. On the two occasions when small acreages did come up for bid, the price was way over my budget. Nevertheless, attending auctions was a good way of meeting land owners, as well as picking up useful information.

At the conclusion of one sale, I walked up to the auctioneer and told him I was looking for a small piece of cheap land. Did inexpensive properties, I asked, ever come up for sale on the Rock or Grass Rivers?

"Not very often," he said. "If you find one, the price will be affected by three things: how close it is to town, how good the access to the property is, and the availability of water and utilities."

When I mentioned to a friend a few days later that small properties were seldom auctioned off, she had a suggestion about what I should do next.

## CHAPTER SIXTEEN

# SURPLUS
# GOVERNMENT LAND

"Check out the federal government," said a friend of mine I ran into at the coffee shop. "I hear they sometimes sell off surplus land."

It seemed unlikely that the federal government would be selling the type of land I was looking for, but I nevertheless decided to investigate.

At the public library I discovered that, for $1.00, I could obtain a twelve-page pamphlet entitled, *Are There Any Public Lands for Sale?* *

I sent away for the pamphlet. When it arrived I learned that the BLM (the Bureau of Land Management, which is part of the U.S. Department of Interior) occasionally sells undeveloped property it no longer needs. This property is sold by competitive bidding at public auction, and by law can not be sold at less than fair market value. However, Iowa was listed among the twenty-two states which had no public lands managed by the BLM.

Surplus federal land is also auctioned off by the GSA (General Services Administration) which maintains a computerized list of available properties. Anyone with access to a personal computer

---

* Available from the U.S. Consumer Information Center, P.O. Box 100, Pueblo, CO 81002, or from any Bureau of Land Management Office.

and modem can call up the Federal Real Estate System Bulletin Board and browse through the listings of unused properties held by the GSA, the U.S. Postal Service, and the Defense Department.*

I logged onto the board with my computer, but found no listings for property in Iowa. However, the search got me thinking. How about looking for property at a tax sale?

* A sixteen-page pamphlet, *U.S. Real Property Sales List*, is available at no charge from the U.S. Consumer Information Center. The current telephone number of the bulletin board is listed on the back page of the *Sales List*. The number can also be obtained from any GSA office.

## CHAPTER SEVENTEEN

# TAX SALES

*Me:* What do you think about looking for a piece of country property at a tax sale?

I was talking to Diane, a friend of mine who had been a real estate agent in California a few years earlier.

*Diane:* It's kind of like trying to win the lottery. It's very unlikely that an owner would let his property go for back taxes.

*Me:* I've read about it happening, though.

*Diane:* Oh, it happens occasionally. But think about it. Why would anybody in their right mind neglect to pay their taxes, then walk away and abandon the property?

*Me:* Maybe they don't have money for taxes.

*Diane:* No, that doesn't make sense. Let's say someone owns a piece of rural property that's worth $15,000. He owes $1,000 in back taxes, but he's broke. Sure, he *could* abandon the property. But what else could he do?

*Me:* Sell it?

*Diane:* Exactly. The property's worth $15,000, so even if he sold it at a sacrifice price – say $10,000 – he'd still end up with $9,000 in his pocket after the taxes were paid.

*Me:* Maybe there's a mortgage which hasn't been paid off. Maybe he has so little equity in the property that, even if he can sell it for $10,000, he won't walk away with any money.

*Diane:* That's unlikely, since lenders – banks – usually collect not only the loan payments, but also the property taxes, which the bank then pays to the county. The bank doesn't want the property sold at auction.

*Me:* But apparently people *do* buy property at tax sales, occasionally.

*Diane:* Sure. But if you purchase land at a tax sale, and it doesn't get redeemed* after the sale, you should ask yourself, "Why, for good–ness sake, is this happening? What's wrong with the property?"

*Me:* What do you mean?

*Diane:* I knew a situation where a married couple bought a mom-and-pop grocery store at a tax sale. They thought they had gotten it real cheap. Then they found out it used to be an automobile service station, and by golly, they discovered there was a leaking gasoline tank deep in the ground. As the new owners of the property, they were now responsible for cleaning up the toxic

---

* In Iowa, even after a property is sold for back taxes, the previous owner has one year during which he can redeem the property by paying the back taxes, plus interest and costs. During this period, the purchaser can't move onto the property, or use it in any way. If the property is redeemed, the purchaser gets back whatever he paid for the property, plus interest. The statutory redemption period varies from state to state.

mess. It cost them thousands and thousands of dollars, much more than they had saved by buying the "bargain" at the tax sale.

*Me:* So you just have to check out the property before the sale. Make sure there are no hazardous wastes.

*Diane:* There can be other problems. For instance, maybe there's a title dispute. The point is, if the owner's going to abandon it, that in itself should indicate that there's probably something wrong with the property. I would be very cautious in going to a tax sale and trying to get something for nothing. You could end up with a bunch of liability that you didn't even know you were getting into.

I was still intrigued, however, so I paid a visit to the Treasurer's Office at the Columbia County Courthouse to find out about the local situation. According to the treasurer, more than ninety-nine per cent of the properties which are sold, eventually get redeemed. In other words, seldom does a purchaser actually acquire title to a property.*

I decided to forget about tax sales, and instead, try another real estate broker.

---

* Most people who purchase property at tax sales in Iowa aren't interested in acquiring land. Instead, they're seeking a short-term investment of their money. The tax delinquent land owner is charged a penalty by the county of two percent interest per month from the time the property is sold, and this money is eventually turned over to the buyer. Because the buyer receives this interest even if the property is redeemed, the yield of twenty-four percent per year makes tax sale purchases very attractive.

## Chapter Eighteen

# ANOTHER BROKER

This time I visited a broker who ran his business out of an old grocery store on the outskirts of Springfield. When I entered the office, the broker was playing solitaire at his desk.

> *Me:* Could I look through your listings?  I'm interested in five to twenty wooded acres in the country, without a house.  I don't have much to spend, maybe $5,000.

He looked at me and smiled, but didn't say a word.

> *Me:* Is it hard to find a small acreage?

> *Broker:* It's worse than that!

> *Me:* Do you have any small parcels at all?

> *Broker:* Actually, there is a place you should look at.  Seven acres with a small... it's not really a house.  More like a shack.

> *Me:* Where is it?

> *Broker:* About twelve miles southwest of Spring-field on a paved road.  It's got utilities, so you could pull a mobile home on the lot and move right in.

> *Me:* I don't need a place to live, just some woods to escape to on the weekend.  I'd prefer a gravel road because there's less road noise.

*Broker:* Gravel roads don't get plowed good in winter.

*Me:* What's the price?

*Broker:* $18,000.

*Me:* The problem is, I want to spend only $5,000 or so.

*Broker:* Well, the seller is *asking* eighteen. Make him an offer.

*Me:* If he's asking eighteen, I doubt if he'll accept five. Do you have any listings in Fillmore County? I've heard that land prices are cheaper down there.

*Broker:* Oh, you mean down in Lapland?

*Me:* Lapland?

*Broker:* Yeah. Fillmore County is down there right next to the state line, where Iowa sort of laps over into Missouri. We call that Lapland. Those people are different down there.

*Me:* Different? In what way?

*Broker:* Well, for one thing, they take it easy down there. Real easy.

*Me:* What do you mean?

*Broker:* Ask them where a property line is, more than likely they'll say, "Over there... or maybe it's over here." Yep, they take it real easy. I heard that if you took all them Laplanders and sent them back to Missouri, you'd raise the I. Q. of both states by ten per cent.

He keep a straight face for about four seconds, then burst out laughing.

> *Me:* Is land really cheaper in Fillmore County?
>
> *Broker:* Oh, maybe a little. But watch out. Court records aren't kept good down there. It's real messed up.

The conversation got me thinking. In an attempt to find out whether land prices were really lower in Fillmore County, I visited the Iowa State University Extension agent in Springfield.*

The county agent gave me a pamphlet reporting the comparative values of land in the state, county by county.

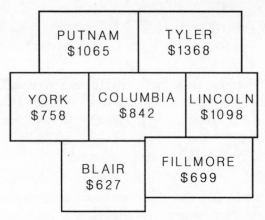

In the seven counties within my target area, the average price of agricultural land ranged from $627 per acre to $1,368 per acre. In Fillmore County, the average price per acre was $699.

However, it was questionable how relevant this $699 figure was to my search. The statistics in the pamphlet were for agricultural land, and the number of acres in the average farm was much larger than the 5- to 20-acre parcel I was looking for.

* Each county in Iowa has an extension agent who assists local farmers.

If I had been looking for a typical 200- or 300-acre farm in Fillmore County, the $699 figure might be useful as a yardstick. But since I wanted a much smaller parcel, I'd undoubtedly have to spend more than $699 per acre. On the other hand, I was looking for land with timber on it, which usually goes for considerably less than prime crop land.

The pamphlet's figures were meaningful in one respect, though. There was no doubt that agricultural land was cheaper in Fillmore County than in Columbia County, and it seemed likely that the same might hold true for a small parcel of recreational land.

\* \* \* \*

So far, the real estate agents I had talked to were based in Springfield. I decided to try one of the brokerages in Fillmore County.

"I'm looking for five to twenty rural acres, real cheap," I said to the middle-aged fellow behind the desk. He ran a small real estate office in Warrensburg, Fillmore County's largest town. "Just bare land," I said. "No need for a house. I don't want to pay the taxes for a building that I don't need."

"If taxes are important," he said, "don't buy anything smaller than ten acres. Less than that, the tax rate is higher. If you've got the time, I'll show you some properties."

He drove me out to see two parcels. One was a 6-acre property with a cabin. The building was so close to the road that there wouldn't be any privacy, and the asking price was $20,000. The other parcel consisted of twenty acres of pasture for $11,000. Although neither property was suitable, his suggestion regarding taxes and parcel size was intriguing. I decided to find out if what he said was true.

At the courthouse the assessor confirmed that, at least in

Fillmore County, ten acres marked the cut-off point. If a parcel is less than ten acres, it's presumed to be residential. As such, it's taxed at the residential rate, which is relatively high. If, however, a parcel is ten acres or more, it's presumed to be agricultural, and thus is taxed at one of the agricultural rates, which are relatively low.*

The friendliness and helpfulness shown by the agent in Warrensburg got me thinking about brokers. Maybe it would be a good idea, I decided, to visit some of the real estate agents in a few of the other small towns in the area.

However, since at that time I was involved in a work project which was consuming most of my time, I decided to write to the brokers rather than visit them personally. I composed a letter saying that I was looking for ten to forty acres, then mailed it to four brokers. None of them ever contacted me.

I assumed that I had gotten no response because the brokers didn't have any appropriate properties. However, there might have been another explanation. A year and a half later, well after I had found and purchased my property, I read something on this very point in a *Harrowsmith Magazine* article.**

The author said that it was silly to merely leave your name with an agent, along with a description of the type of property you're looking for, and expect him to get back to you when he finds something suitable. Chances are, your request will be filed and forgotten.

Instead, the author suggested, keep pestering the agent. Every time you visit him, ask to see his new listings. Eventually he

* I've discovered that the rules vary from county to county.
** *The Good, the Bad, and the Swampy*, by Kathlyn Poff. *Harrowsmith Magazine*, number 12, volume 2:6 (1978). The article was later reprinted in a book, *The Harrowsmith Reader*, edited by James Lawrence and published by Camden House in 1978.

may show you something special.

However, even if I had read that article back in 1992, it probably wouldn't have persuaded me that all I had to do was keep pestering the brokers. I had come to the conclusion that, to find a cheap piece of property which met my criteria, I'd have to do the leg work myself.

The problem, though, was time. I had no idea how long it would take to find a suitable property. Maybe, I said to myself, I should simultaneously be looking for a tractor, in case that also took a long time.

## Chapter Nineteen

# TRACTOR ADVICE

*Kim:* Believe it or not, Ralph, a big tractor's going to be cheaper than a small one.

*Me:* Why is that?

*Kim:* There's a greater demand for small tractors, partly because they're favored by people who live in town. A home owner can mow grass with a small, light tractor which won't tear up the lawn. A bigger, heavier model would sink into the grass. Also, antique tractor collectors seem to covet the small units, possibly because fewer of them were made. For whatever reason, demand for small tractors has pushed up the price.

Kim was a friend who lived in the country. Although he didn't farm, he owned a tractor, and he seemed to know a lot about them.

*Me:* I'd even settle for an old junker. All I need is something to haul things around with.

*Kim:* Make sure the tires are in serviceable condition. New tires for the rear can cost hundreds of dollars a piece, and if a tractor has been sitting outdoors for a long time, its tires may have deteriorated. The sun wears them out. Also, try to find a tractor with a universal, 3-point hitch. You'll then be able to use implements from many different tractor manufacturers, not just those from your brand of tractor. And try to get a tractor with a wide front end. It'll be less likely to tip over than one with a "tricycle" front end.

*Me:* How much will I have to spend?

*Kim:* Eight hundred dollars, maybe.

*Me:* Any tips on checking it out before I buy it?

*Kim:* Pay attention to all the things you'd check on a used car, then drive it around and listen for noises. Make sure the hydraulics work.

I started by looking at the "Farm Related" classified ad section in our local newspaper, but weeks went by without a single tractor being listed. It turned out that the *Des Moines Register*, the state's largest paper, was where the greatest amount of farm equipment was advertised.

In each Sunday edition, hundreds of ads for tractors and implements appeared. However, most of the listings were for relatively new tractors, not more than ten or fifteen years old, and all of them were very expensive. It wasn't uncommon to see these tractors priced at $40,000, $50,000, and up. Occasionally, there would be an ad for an older tractor at $700 or $800, but invariably the seller was located in another part of the state. I didn't want to drive more than forty or fifty miles to pick up a tractor.

Tractor dealers seemed the next logical place to look, but none of the dealerships I called had any inexpensive, older models. It was at the farm auctions, though, that I started seeing some likely prospects.

All types of tractors were sold at the local auctions, from units in good condition to those that were barely running. Occasionally, even a tractor with a seized motor came up for sale.

Sometimes, a running tractor would sell for $600 or $700, but I always held back from bidding. I wanted to drive a tractor before I bought it, and although the engines of the tractors at auctions were started up before the bidding commenced, there was never a chance to actually drive the units around. I was worried that, even if the motor sounded good, the tractor might have a bad transmission, clutch, or rear end.

However, I learned a lot at the auctions. At one sale, I pulled the dip stick out of an engine to check the oil. Instead of clean new oil, or even black, contaminated oil, the dip stick was covered with a frothy gray mixture of water and oil, indicating that something was seriously wrong with the engine. When the tractor was started up just before the bidding commenced, though, the engine sounded ok, and the winning bid was fairly high.

The more auctions I attended, the more I got a feel for tractor prices. All John Deere equipment brought top dollar. The same was true for the Ford "N" series tractors. The Farmall and Allis Chalmers tractors, on the other hand, sold more reasonably.

Although I attended every farm machinery auction I could, I decided not only to hold out for a tractor I could test drive, but for one which could be bought for $500 or less.

As it turned out, it wouldn't be long before I stumbled onto something promising. It would be a piece of property, though, not a tractor.

## CHAPTER TWENTY

# THE
# COST OF WATER

It was late at night and I was tired, but the plat book was fascinating. I was propped up in bed with two pillows behind my back, and I was having so much fun that I didn't want to go to sleep.

I was scanning the pages, looking for small tracts of land. Most of the parcels were between 80 and 320 acres, but occasionally I'd spot a 10- or 20-acre tract. When I did, I'd look to see what kind of road it was on. The plat maps differentiated among paved, gravel, and dirt roads, and I was holding out for a property on a gravel road.

Some of the parcels were landlocked. In other words, they didn't abut any roads. An owner of such a property would have to drive over a neighbor's land in order to get to his own parcel. I didn't want landlocked property, even if the appropriate easement existed over a neighbor's land, since I didn't like the idea of muddy or snowy trips across farmland every time I visited my property.

While looking at the plat of one of the northeastern townships in Columbia County, a 10-acre parcel caught my eye. The property was located at a spot where the county road made a 90-degree turn. The map indicated that the road was gravel up to the bend in the road where the property was, but beyond that point the road was dirt.

It's not uncommon for roads in Iowa to start out gravel, then turn to dirt. The situation usually results because of the lack of houses beyond a certain point in the road. The county road department will dump gravel on the road up to the last house, but they're not willing to maintain a road on which nobody lives.

As I studied the plat, I realized that there could be an advantage in owning property at such a spot. There'd be little or no traffic in front of the property, since few people venture down a dirt road. But because of the gravel, I'd still be able to get to the property in wet weather.

The plat map also indicated that a creek ran along the back edge of the 10-acre parcel. Getting out of bed, I went and found the topographical map for that area. Although the topo map didn't show property boundaries, it was easy to locate the road with the bend in it. The topo map, just like the plat book, was divided into townships and sections, and the 10-acre parcel happened to be located in the exact corner of one of the sections.

Green ink markings on the topo map showed that the whole parcel, as well as the surrounding area, was wooded, but the map also revealed another interesting fact. There weren't any dots to indicate nearby houses. In fact, it looked as if the closest building was one mile away. I noticed, however, that the map had been created in 1980, so I realized that other buildings might have been erected since then. As I drifted off to sleep, I pictured myself tracking down the owner of the property and discovering that he was desperate to sell.

The following evening I drove out to the property. After parking the car, I got out and walked along the road. It was hot, and whip-poor-wills were singing in the trees. Just as the map had indicated, the land on both sides of the road was timber. On the 10-acre parcel's side, the land was fenced.

About 100 feet down the road was an opening in the fence. Strands of barbed wire were strung between two large fence posts, and a driveway had been graded from the county road through the posts.

There were no electric poles running down the county road, and no pedestals or markers for phone or rural water. The place looked promising, and during the drive back home I noticed that electricity poles were strung to, but stopped at, the closest farmhouse, which was a mile away from the 10-acre parcel.

The next day I visited the Columbia County courthouse. At the assessor's office, I pointed out on a map the parcel I was interested in, and the clerk, after checking her records, gave me the name and address of the owner. The address was in Des Moines, sixty miles from Springfield. I also asked for the book and page number where the deed was recorded.

At the recorder's office, I gave the clerk the book and page number, and requested a photocopy of the deed. At the top of the document there was stamped a notation that $3.85 in transfer tax had been paid at the time of sale, which occurred in 1976. The clerk, after referring to a chart, said that meant the property had been bought for $4,000.

Next, I went to the public library, where I found a Des Moines telephone book. It contained a listing for the owner of the land, and that night I gave him a call.

> *Me:* I was wondering if you might consider selling the property.
>
> *Owner:* Well, I hadn't thought about it, and it really belongs to our children, so I'd have to talk to them. How much were you thinking of spending?

I hated to be asked that question. Although I *had* thought

about an amount I'd be willing to spend ($5,000 to $8,000), it didn't seem like good negotiating strategy to disclose this figure to a seller. Therefore, I always tried to avoid answering any questions about how much I could spend.

> *Me:* I'm not sure what a 10-acre parcel should
> be worth. Do you mind if I go out and
> walk around the land?

> *Owner:* No, go ahead.

After returning to the property the next day, I climbed over the strands of barbed wire and followed the driveway up the hill. I could see from the untrampled grass on the drive that there hadn't been any vehicles on the property recently.

At the top of the hill the driveway opened into a clearing. As I walked around the opening in the trees, I looked for evidence that, in the past, a building or trailer had been located there. There weren't, however, any foundations, trash, or holes in the ground.

A slight breeze started to blow, and as I listened to the wind whistle in the trees, I became aware of another sound. Frogs! In the distance, frogs were croaking.

*If there are frogs, there's probably water.*

Heading in the direction of the sound, I walked further into the property. The land sloped downward from the clearing, and after winding my way through about twenty feet of short evergreen trees, I came to a large pond. I stepped onto a rock at the water's edge and heard a splash a few feet away as a frog jumped into the water.

I estimated that the pond, which was rectangular, was roughly 60 by 150 feet in size. It was surrounded by trees on two sides, and on three sides the land sloped up sharply from the water's edge.

*This is beautiful, much better than most of the farm ponds I've seen, which are usually on flat land with no trees.*

It was also secluded. Because of the hill between the road and the pond, the water wasn't visible to anyone driving by.

I noted the condition of the pond, which had been created by filling in the low end of a natural gully with earth, creating a dam. In the middle of the dam was a concrete spillway which allowed excess water to flow over the dam without eroding it.

After examining the dam, I started walking around the rest of the pond.

*Where does the water for the pond come from?*

It was obvious that the pond contained runoff. As I continued my walk, I realized that most of the water came down a long hill on the west side of the pond.

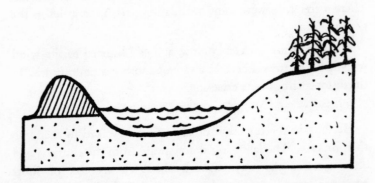

That hill continued upwards another 300 or 400 feet and onto the neighboring property, where corn was growing.

*Wow. Most of the water comes down that hill from the field, which is farmed. That means chemicals. I bet this water if full of pesticides and fertilizers.*

Although the pond looked clean, if the soil in the cornfield had chemicals in it, then the pond water certainly wasn't fit for drinking, maybe not even for bathing or swimming.

The remaining part of the property was all timber, and the further I went from the road, the higher the land got. At the back of the parcel the ground dropped off abruptly to a stream below.

As I climbed down the cliff, I noticed that cows were grazing near the stream, which meandered and was about six feet wide. A fence, overrun with brush and vines, ran between the creek and the 10-acre parcel. In other words, the creek was on the adjoining property.

*Even if the stream was on the 10-acre parcel, the water wouldn't be safe for drinking. It's obvious from the hoof prints in the bank that the cows wander in and out of the stream.*

After climbing back up the cliff, I explored the remainder of the property. Although the timbered area of the parcel was pretty, I was beginning to realize that the lack of pure water was the property's main drawback.

Actually, water wouldn't be an immediate need. Since I wouldn't be living on the land, I could always haul in whatever water I needed. Nevertheless, I realized that the availability of water would be critical if I ever decided to sell the parcel. Drilling a well didn't appeal to me, since I had read that more and more wells were becoming contaminated.

After returning home, I called the municipal water department in Springfield and found out the name of the rural water district that the 10-acre parcel was located in.

When I reached the rural water company, the first thing the engineer asked for was the township and section where the property was located. He had a plat map in front of him, and he quickly located the property.

*Engineer:* We don't have a pipe running down that dirt road, and the closest service is roughly two miles south.

*Me:* How much would it cost to get water to the property?

*Engineer:* I can only give you a rough estimate, but to extend the main – that's two inch pipe – we're talking $2.00 per foot. That's assuming we don't have to do any right-of-way clearing with a dozer. Then to go underneath the road with the main, $20.00 per foot, and usually it's a fifty to seventy foot bore. Once you get to the property, you've got costs for the meter pit, your membership, and hook-up fees.

*Me:* If I found another piece of land where the rural water pipe already ran down the road past the property, what would it cost?

*Engineer:* That would depend on which side of the road the pipe was on. A typical "longside" hookup is $1,725.00. That's what we call it when the pipe's on the opposite side of the road. A typical "shortside" is $1,225.00.

The engineer told me the name of the farmer with the closest hookup, and after hanging up the phone, I used my plat and topographical maps to measure the road distance between that farm and the 10-acre parcel. It was 7,000 feet.

At two dollars a foot, that would come to $14,000.00 just to extend the main to the property! I called the owner and told him that, although the property was beautiful, I wanted to continue looking at other parcels.

A few days later I saw a newspaper ad for something cheap. So cheap, in fact, that it seemed almost too good to be true.

## CHAPTER TWENTY-ONE

# BUYING THE TRACTOR

natic, loaded
· Ford truck
four tires.
'00 miles.
,fore 7 a.m
veekends.

· XLT 4X -
and locks
clean truck.
Springfield.

5 BLAZER -
owner, runs

combine - 30.5x32 tires.
chopper, new rotor bars, 2-
speed hydro, all extra
options, excellent condition.
$55,000. 515-555-3786.

FOR SALE - H tractor,
narrow front. Runs and
drives, needs engine work.
$300. 555-2178.

MANURE SPREADER with
end gate. 180 Gehl ex-
cellent condition; 3,250
bhel arc

Chevy
515/555-31

1986 MUS
cylinder, 4
runs good,
left. $1,350

1989 CHRY
- 96K, one
$4,200.
loaded, pc
locks. 555

I saw the ad in the *Allentown News*, a newspaper published twenty-five miles west of Springfield. I immediately called the telephone number and a woman answered.

*Woman:* No, the tractor ain't sold yet.

    *Me:* What make is it?

*Woman:* Farmall. Farmall H.

*Me:* The ad says the engine needs work. What
does that mean?

*Woman:* Well... you know how some tractors smoke
a little?

*Me:* Yes.

*Woman:* Well, this tractor smokes *a lot!*

The woman said that her husband would be back around
eight that night, and I promised to call back then. In the
meantime, I needed to do some research. I had heard of the H
model Farmalls, but I wanted to find out more about them.

Our public library had a large reference book dealing with
tractors, and in it I learned that the International Harvester
Company, which manufactured Farmalls, had made 391,230
model H tractors between 1939 and 1953. The H, a 5-speed row
crop tractor that produced 19.1 drawbar and 24.3 belt horse-
power, weighed 3,784 pounds and sold for $962 on full rubber.
(It was also available on steel wheels.)

I called the husband that evening.

*Me:* What condition is the rubber in?

*Farmer:* It's acceptable.

*Me:* Do all the gears and the clutch work?

*Farmer:* Yes.

*Me:* Could I come over now and look at it?

*Farmer:* Sure can. I'm not going anywhere.

His farm was about fifty miles away, and I got there a little
after ten that night. It was raining hard, and it was cold. As my
Datsun turned into his driveway, the car's headlights shined on
the tractor, which was sitting out in the rain in front of a barn.
The farmer hadn't heard me arrive, so I had time to look at the
tractor by myself.

Although it was rusty, the tractor looked fairly complete. None of the sheet metal covering the engine and radiator was torn or badly dented. However, when I looked at the engine, I saw a number of things that weren't exactly kosher.

One of the battery cables had been disconnected, and the metal breather pipe that was supposed to connect the air cleaner to the carburetor was missing. A rubber hose that carried fuel from the gas tank was disconnected at the carburetor, and the end of the hose was plugged by a bolt jammed into its end. The wires to the generator weren't connected to anything.

*Boy, it's in horrible shape.*

When I knocked on the farmhouse door, a short, stocky man came out. He looked about forty-five.

> *Me:* How long have you had it, and have you
> used it much?
>
> *Farmer:* I bought it a couple of years ago. We got

105

hogs, and I use it to haul manure.
Mowing, utility work.

*Me:* I'd like to hear it run.

*Farmer:* Sure. Here's how to start it. First you
remove the bolt from the gas line, like this.
Then connect the hose to the carb.

*Me:* Why is the bolt jammed in the fuel line
like that?

*Farmer:* Well, otherwise the gas leaks out the carb
all night long. Like I said, connect the gas
line, then turn the petcock under the tank.
Snap the ignition switch on, bolt on the
battery strap, then put your hand over this
choke thing on the carb.

He performed each of these steps as he talked, using the palm
of his left hand to cover the air intake opening of the carburetor.
Holding his left hand in place, he reached back with his right
hand and pressed the starter button. The motor turned over for
about four seconds, then caught. As the engine coughed and
sputtered, he slid his left hand off the carburetor a little, allowing
more air in.

*Farmer:* You got to trick her a little like this 'til she
gets going.

As the engine warmed up, I listened to see if it made any
strange noises. Although it was running rough, I didn't hear
any unusual sounds.

*Me:* Have you had to do much work to it since
you've owned it?

*Farmer:* Heck no. Why, I haven't even had to
change the oil.

*Me:* It doesn't look like the generator's

connected. How do you keep the battery charged?

*Farmer:* It don't take much to start her, so the battery stays juiced up for weeks. When it's out o' pep, I just put the battery in the Camero and drive the car around a bit to charge it up.

*Me:* I'm definitely interested, but I'd like to drive it. Since it doesn't have any lights, and since it's so dark out, could I come back tomorrow morning and drive it up the road? I want to run it through all the gears.

*Farmer:* Sure, whatever. But I'll tell you right now, I ain't gonna dicker. I paid $300 for it two years ago, and that's what I want. If it's worth $300 to you, it's yours. If not, I'll just keep it. Three hundred, cash.

He showed me how to shift into each of the five forward gears, as well as reverse, and as I drove home in the rain that night, it was hard to contain my excitement. A tractor for $300! And one that ran! Along with the excitement, though, I felt fear. What if this 50-year old monster turned out to be a mechanic's nightmare?

The next morning, after getting $300 in bills at my bank's drive-through window, I returned to the farm. I arrived about 8:30, but the farmer wasn't there. His wife, standing in the kitchen door, said I could start up the tractor myself.

Before cranking it over, I drained a few drops of oil from one of the petcocks on the side of the crankcase. Although the oil was pitch black, it didn't look as if water had gotten in the oil. If an engine has a cracked block, water from the cooling system can get into the crankcase, which will make the oil frothy and gray.

When I pressed the starter button, the engine came to life just as quickly as it had the night before. As I climbed onto the seat, I realized I was more excited than I had been when I had driven a car for the first time at age fifteen. No car's engine was ever so beautifully loud as this, and no seat so high in the air. As I slipped the transmission into first gear and the tractor lurched forward, a big grin appeared on my face.

After making a few turns on the soggy grass, I shifted into second gear and drove onto the county highway. As soon as I gave the engine more gas, I heard and felt a very loud thump. After about two seconds, there was another thump, then another. The noise seemed to be coming from the front wheels, and the jarring was so severe that I could actually feel it through the seat and steering wheel. I stopped the tractor, climbed down, and looked at the front tires to see if there was something wrong with the front axle.

The tractor had two small wheels in front, and when I looked closely, I saw that one of the tires didn't have a valve stem. There was no air inside that tire, but I hadn't noticed it earlier because the other tire was apparently overinflated. Or was it?

As I examined the inflated tire, I noticed that it was slightly flat on one side. I kicked the tire, but it didn't give at all. It was hard as a brick. Then I noticed a hole in the tread of the tire about the diameter of a silver dollar. The hole was plugged up with.... cement.

*Heck, this whole tire is filled with cement.*

I climbed back on the tractor and ran it through the remaining gears. They all worked, and I didn't hear any transmission or rear-end noises. However, the thumping noise from the front end was terrible.

After driving back to the farmhouse, I climbed down and

proceeded to examine the tractor more carefully. As I was checking out the rear tires, a pick-up truck drove into the yard. A tall man in his fifties, dressed in denim overalls, got out and came over to the tractor. "Is this the tractor that's for sale?" he said.

I tensed up. What if he offered more than $300 for it? "Uh, it was," I said, "but I've already bought it. I mean... "

I turned away and walked quickly to the farmhouse. The farmer's wife invited me into the kitchen, and I took out my wallet. I handed her the money quickly and said I'd call her husband about picking up the tractor.

During the drive back home in my Datsun, I couldn't stop laughing.

*I've got a tractor, I've got a tractor!*

Now all I needed was a place to store it.

The next day I paid $25 to a commercial storage company for a month's rent on a 12x16-foot garage. It was November and the weather would soon turn cold, and I needed a sheltered place with electricity where I could work on the tractor. I paid an acquaintance $50 to pick up the Farmall with his flatbed truck, and as soon as the tractor was in the storage space, I went to work on it.

The tractor's starter needed rebuilding, which cost $18. I replaced the 6-volt generator with a used alternator from an automobile, and bought a new 12-volt battery. While rebuilding the carburetor, I got the choke to work properly, and by replacing the worn-out pet cock that shuts off the gas at the tank, I was able to get rid of the make-shift bolt from the gas line. The engine still smoked a lot, but since it started well, I decided to postpone an overhaul until I had a permanent place to store the tractor.

Over the next few weeks I mentioned to everyone I met that I wanted to rent space in a barn, which I figured would cost less than the storage area. A lady who helped my mother with the housework suggested I talk to her friend, Daryl, who lived on a farm fifteen miles out in the country. I had never met him, but I went down to his farm one night and introduced myself.

*Daryl:* Sure, you can put it in one of the sheds.

    *Me:* How much do you want per month?

*Daryl:* Ahh, it'd be too much trouble to get paid for it. The space is just sitting there, so you're welcome to it.

    *Me:* If you ever need help with anything, let me know.

*Daryl:* Now that you mention it, I could use some help come haying time.

A few days later I called the farmer who had sold me the tractor. I asked him about the cement. "Well," he said, "the front tires kept getting punctured by thorns. I got so tired of replacing tubes that I filled one of the tires with cement. Never had a lick of trouble after that!"

About a week later, after choosing a route over back-country gravel roads, I drove the tractor down to Daryl's farm. Even in fifth gear, top speed was only fifteen miles per hour, and it took almost an hour to get there.

As I backed the tractor into one of his sheds, Daryl yelled to me, "You're sort of doing it ass-backward, aren't you?"

"You mean I should pull it in frontwards?" I asked.

"No," he said. "It's just that most people would buy the land first, *then* get the tractor."

CHAPTER TWENTY-TWO

# THE
# DEAD END ROAD

It was a Saturday morning, and as I drove down a stretch of winding county road, I kept my eyes open for interesting spots. Old, abandoned farmhouses or barns especially intrigued me, since their neglect might indicate a willingness on the part of the owners to sell.

This particular road ran through rolling, timbered country in Blair County. At the top of one of the hills I noticed a narrow driveway which branched off from the main county road. Stopping the car, I opened the plat map to see where the side road went. The map showed it extending south for a quarter mile, then dead ending.

As I pulled the Datsun onto the smaller road, I spotted an electrical utility line which ran on one side of the road, indicating that there had to be at least one customer further on down.

Both sides of the roadway were timbered. After about a quarter of a mile I came to a barbed wire fence across the road. Beyond the fence, grass-covered ruts continued up and over a hill, suggesting that the road had originally gone further.

Stopping the car, I looked to the east. Just barely visible beyond a number of huge trees was a building. It looked as if it had originally been a one-room cabin, onto which three rooms and a garage had been added. However, the additions were more like lean-tos, and the whole thing looked pretty junky. The building wasn't painted, and some of the siding had fallen partly off and was hanging at odd angles.

Two tire ruts, leading from the road to the garage, were covered with a string of 2x8-inch boards. Somebody had apparently found it easier to drive to the garage over the boards rather than sink into the wet grass.

*It's run down, but I doubt if anybody ever comes down this road, so it'd be real private.*

I was itching to walk around the building and explore, but I didn't want to trespass. Some grass in front of the structure looked as if it had been recently mowed, but other than that, there was no sign that the place was occupied. There weren't any cars, trucks, or farm machinery anywhere, but I did notice that an electric service line ran to the building.

It started to rain, and as I sat in the Datsun listening to the sound of the raindrops on the car's roof, I imagined what it would be like to own the property.

*The building is nestled back under the trees, so it's protected from the sun.*

After returning home, I got my plat book out and discovered that the building sat on a 424-acre parcel owned by an "A. McGowan." No one was shown as living on the parcel, though, and the index at the back of the plat book didn't list the home address of the owner.

During a visit to the library in Stillwater a few days later, I happened to mention to the librarian that I had found an interesting property owned by A. McGowan. "Oh," she said, "that'd be old Judge McGowan. He retired years ago and now farms." He lived in a small town in an adjoining county, she said, as she looked up his phone number and address for me.

Although I wanted to contact him immediately, I decided not to telephone. I figured that it would be easier for him to say "no" over the phone than in person. Also, it would be more fun to meet him face to face.

I didn't have any trouble finding the Judge's home, but when I knocked on the door there wasn't any answer. In fact, I had to return to the house five more times before I finally caught him at home.

> *Me:* I want to buy a small acreage, and I'm interested in a piece of property I think you own.
>
> *Judge:* I don't know whether I want to sell, but I'll be glad to talk.

He invited me in, and we sat down at his dining room table. He was tall, thin, and probably in his late sixties. I pulled my plat book out from my back pocket and showed him the property.

> *Me:* The place intrigues me because it's so isolated. Is there any chance you'd want to break off ten or twenty acres, including the cabin?
>
> *Judge:* Well, I might, but not now. There's somebody living out there.
>
> *Me:* Oh, a renter?
>
> *Judge:* No, not exactly. Do you know Mr. Peters?
>
> *Me:* I don't think so.
>
> *Judge:* He owned that place for years, lived out there. He got pretty feeble, so he sold it to me, then ended up in the county home. But he didn't stay there long. Said he couldn't stand being cooped up. So he's

back out at the cabin. I don't take any rent from him, and I won't sell the place while he's still alive. I haul water out to him once a month.

Me: How about if I give you a call in a year or so, if I'm still looking for a place. I'm not in a big hurry.

Judge: Ok. You know, there's a log house for sale north of there, over on the Rock River. It's a year-round house, and I think they might take $40,000 for it.

I looked up at his face and saw that he was staring me right in the eyes. The thought came to me that he was studying my face to see how I'd react to the mention of $40,000. I told him that was much more than I wanted to spend, and that, anyway, I didn't need a property with a house on it.

As it turned out, in a few weeks I was to learn about a piece of river land that *was* cheap. Real cheap.

## CHAPTER TWENTY-THREE

# TOO MUCH WATER

building. Six car garage, new roof, needs work. Rural water, new furnace. 319-555-3625.

- Collection orts cards. 98.

TV - And ?. both in . Sell only $250. xringfield.

oat straw.

FOR SALE: Approximately 6 acres of ground on the Grass River near Smith's Landing. $4,000. 319-555-5503.

FOR SALE - Beautifully preserved older house, with wood cabinets, new carpet.

THURSDAY. 10:00 a.m. Consignmer Located ea Sharon, la & Hwy. 66. C 319-555-2!

SATURDAY P.M. - Real acres m/l east of Re west of C land

When I saw the classified ad, which appeared in *The Springfield Gazette*, I took a pen and used the white space in the newspaper's margin to figure out the price per acre. In my excitement, I forgot which numbers to divide into which, and when my calculation indicated that the price was $1,500 per acre, I switched the figures around and divided *quantity* into price.

That calculation produced a figure of $666.66 per acre.

Four thousand dollars was a price I could easily handle, and riverfront land was hard to find. I had been looking for property for the past six months, and this was only the second riverfront acreage I had come across that was up for sale.

During the next three days I tried reaching the owner by telephone, but I never got an answer. Finally, on the fourth day, I called at 6:30 A.M and caught him in. He sounded wide awake and cheerful.

> *Me:* Do people live right next to the property? I'm sort of looking for a secluded place.
>
> *Owner:* Oh, there are no close neighbors.
>
> *Me:* What kind of road is it on?
>
> *Owner:* Gravel.
>
> *Me:* How much road frontage is there?
>
> *Owner:* Lots.
>
> *Me:* Is the property rectangular in shape?
>
> *Owner:* No, not really. More like a triangle.
>
> *Me:* Is it fenced?
>
> *Owner:* Nope.
>
> *Me:* Would it have to be surveyed?
>
> *Owner:* Nope.
>
> *Me:* How would I know where the boundaries are?
>
> *Owner:* I know where they are. I'll show you.

We made arrangements to meet the next day at 6 P.M. in front of the old church in Smith's Landing. The building wasn't hard to find, since it was the only church in the small town of 117 residents.

The owner was in his late thirties and was accompanied by his wife. They headed off to the property in a pickup truck, with me following in my Datsun.

After traveling about one mile on a paved road we turned off onto the "gravel" road. The pickup kicked up a huge cloud of dust, and after a few seconds I no longer could see the vehicle in front of me.

However, there was just enough visibility to the side for me to notice two road signs on the right. One sign read, "CAUTION, MINIMUM MAINTENANCE ROAD." The other warned, "LEVEL B SERVICE. ENTER AT YOUR OWN RISK."

*This isn't gravel, it's dirt!*

The road wound through flat land planted with corn, and after about a mile we came to a spot where the river ran parallel to the road. At a bend in the road, the owner pulled off to the side and we all got out.

*Owner:* The east boundary is over by that big tree.

As we climbed down from the road and waded into deep grass, I was glad I had put my high rubber boots on. The ground was wet and soggy, and my feet sunk into the mud a few inches.

*Me:* How do you know the east boundary is by

that tree?

*Owner:* The guy I bought it from told me. There's
no question about it. Don't worry, you
won't need to have it surveyed.

The owner slapped the side of his neck with the palm of his
hand.

*Owner:* Those mosquitos sure make a bee-line to
me.

I felt a tiny sting on my arm, and as I squashed the insect with
my hand, I noticed that the air was full of mosquitos. Not only
were they starting to bite my face, a couple of them soon got
stuck in my hair and buzzed around on my scalp as they tried to
escape.

The river channel was about 100 feet wide and the water was
running fast. I walked to the edge of the bank, which was about
five feet above the level of the water.

*This part of the property wouldn't be very useful, since it's so close
to the road. There's no privacy at all.*

There were a few large oak trees, but most of the ground was
covered with grass and mud. However, I didn't know where the
property lines were, so I asked the owner if we could walk
around the perimeter of the parcel. As we headed westward
along the river, I noticed that the rushing water had washed
away parts of the river bank, and I had to be careful not to step
too close to the edge, where the earth looked unstable.

*Owner:* The northern property line is over here,
about. There's supposed to be a stake here
somewhere.

*Me:* Does the other boundary of the triangle
follow the river bank?

*Owner:* No. It runs down the middle of the

channel, except that the river has been
slowly moving this way. I couldn't find
that stake here last week, so I think the
river's taken it.

The parcel was on the outer side of a bend in the river, and
erosion was slowly eating away at the property.

It was exciting watching the water rush past, but I had
difficulty picturing what use I could make of the land. The
water was moving too fast to swim in, and I couldn't imagine
wanting a cabin at that spot, since it was so close to the road.

Owner: This is the narrow side of the property.
Do you want to go to the other end?

Me: Sure.

We walked away from the river at an angle and, after a short
distance, came to an area where there were huge logs lying on the
ground. The presence of clean saw cuts on some of the logs
indicated that they had been cut down, but there also were a lot
of trees that looked as if they had been uprooted at the stump. A
few of them were big, at least twenty-five inches in diameter.

Me: Has this place been logged?

Owner: No. These logs are from the river.

Me: You mean when it floods?

Owner: Right.

Me: Does it flood every year?

Owner: Yup.

Me: Well, I guess you never run out of fire
wood.

Owner: That's for sure.

We continued walking in the same general direction, but it
was impossible to keep going in a straight line, since in some

places trees and brush had bunched up into huge piles, some of them at least five feet high. At one spot, the ground was so soggy that my rubber boots, which sank deep in the mud, were hard to pull out.

*Owner:* Here's some deer tracks. Do you hunt?

*Me:* No. But I like the idea of deer running around.

*Owner:* Do you fish?

*Me:* I haven't fished since I was a kid.

The ground was flat, and after about ten minutes we reached the road, which was apparently the property's west boundary.

*Me:* Is there rural water out here?

*Owner:* No, but it's easy to sink a shallow well. You'd get water in ten or twenty feet.

*Me:* Where's the closest electric line?

*Owner:* Down the road and across the bridge.

As we walked along the county road back to the vehicles, we passed a large pile of gravel on the other side of the road that had apparently been dumped there by the county. The top of the pile was light tan in color, but the bottom two feet of rock was brownish.

*Owner:* See that line on the gravel? That was the high water mark of the river.

I looked at the gravel pile, then at the 6-acre property, and the significance of what he was saying sank in. The gravel was higher than the county road, and the county road was higher than the 6-acre parcel, which was flat. Therefore, when the river rose, it not only flooded the whole property, but also the county road as well.

*I couldn't have a cabin, unless it was up on stilts, and I couldn't leave my tractor here. During flood season, I couldn't even drive my car down the road to get to the property.*

All of a sudden, the $4,000 price tag didn't seem so attractive.

That night I sat at the kitchen table and studied my plat books. After a few minutes I found a remote section of country which I hadn't explored yet, and which contained a number of small properties.

The next day, a Saturday, would be perfect for exploring.

## CHAPTER TWENTY-FOUR

# A SUCKER
# FOR OLD BARNS

I stopped my car by the side of a county road in front of an old farmhouse. The roof of the building had caved in, and it was obvious nobody lived there.

As I sat in the driver's seat of my Datsun, trying to find the location of the property on one of my topographical maps, a pickup truck came up the road behind me and stopped next to my car. Sitting at the wheel was an elderly man in denim overalls.

*Owner:* What are you doing here?

*Me:* Just exploring and looking at my map. Why?

*Owner:* I own this place!

I thought of answering, "Do you own the county road too?" But he didn't look friendly, so I held my tongue.

*Me:* Oh, don't worry. I won't go on your land.

I drove off, and about three miles down the road I saw an "Eggs For Sale" sign in front of a freshly-painted farmhouse. Although I didn't need any eggs, I stopped to buy a dozen anyway, since it would provide a good excuse to start a conversation with the farmer. He didn't know of any small acreages for sale, though.

Later that day, while driving down another gravel road, I spotted a small cabin set back in the woods about seventy-five feet from the road. A driveway leading to the building was overgrown with weeds, and there was no sign of anybody around.

After locating the spot on my plat book I discovered that the parcel was ten acres in size. Although I wasn't particularly excited about the land, since the ground was flat and the cabin was too close to the road, I still was curious to find out more about the place.

After obtaining at the courthouse the name and address of the woman who owned the property, I called her that night.

*Me:* Would you be interested in selling?

*Owner:* I don't know. How much you offering?

*Me:* I'd have to walk on the property first to see what it's like. Is it ok if I wander around?

*Owner:* No. I don't want to sell.

Days later I came upon some land that *did* excite me. Or more correctly, a barn on the land excited me. The property was on a little-used gravel road about twenty-five miles from Springfield. The barn was small, only about 16x24 feet, and some of its siding had fallen off. There were no other structures on the property.

That night, after getting in bed and turning the lights out, I devised all sorts of plans for what I'd do with the property if I could buy it. I'd repair the siding on the barn, insulate the walls, and add a wood burning stove.

*Hey, wait a minute. The property's flat and boring, and there aren't any trees. The only reason you like the place is because of the barn. But the fact is, you're a sucker for any old barn.*

I had never admitted this to myself before, but it was true. I

124

*was* a sucker for old barns. Often, it seemed that the more decrepit a barn was, the more pleasure I got in planning how I'd fix it up.

I should be careful, I told myself, to pay more attention to the other features on my wish list and not be swayed by every run-down barn I see.

\*　\*　\*　\*

For the next few weeks I spent most of my free time driving the back roads in Fillmore County. In fact, I covered so many miles that I forgot which stretches of road had already been explored.

To keep from getting confused, I devised a system. I photocopied the pages of the plat book for Fillmore County and kept the copies in my car. Then, whenever I was out driving, I'd stop for a moment every few miles and use a felt pen to color in the route that I had just covered. Even weeks later, all it would take would be a glance at the map to see which roads still remained unexplored.

The more I searched, the more I wondered why it was so difficult to find a small acreage. I decided to ask another friend of mine, Dale, about this.

## CHAPTER TWENTY-FIVE

# WHY SO FEW
# SMALL PARCELS

*Me:* Why is it so hard to find small acreages for sale?

I posed the question to Dale, a farmer I met at one of the meetings of an antique tractor restoration club I had joined.

*Dale:* There are a number of good reasons why a farmer wouldn't want to break off a small part of his holdings.

*Me:* Like what?

*Dale:* For one, many people who live in the country don't want neighbors. They like being away from others.

*Me:* Actually, that's one of the reasons I'm looking for land. I like to be out where nobody else is.

*Dale:* There's another thing. State law limits how many times I can break a parcel into small pieces before I have to contend with the subdivision laws.

*Me:* I never thought of that.

*Dale:* Then there are the expenses.

*Me:* But you'd incur some expenses in any sale,

regardless of the size of the land.

*Dale:* True. But with a small parcel, there's not enough profit. If I sell a large parcel for $120,000, I'll make some money. But if I sell only a few acres for $5,000, it's not worth the time and trouble. And that's not all.

*Me:* What do you mean?

*Dale:* Many of the farms around here have been owned by the same family for generations. Over the years you can get mighty attached to land. It becomes almost like a part of the family. For instance, take my farm. In 1892 – that's over a hundred years ago – my grandpappy built the farmhouse we live in, and he cleared with his own hands the land that I now till. My dad was born in this farmhouse, and I wouldn't sell off a square foot of this farm. Of course, there are ways to get around that obstacle.

*Me:* How?

*Dale:* Buy a big farm from someone who is retiring, a farm with some valuable tillable ground, as well as some rough land or timber. Then sell off the cropland, but keep the timber for yourself. Or rent out the cropland for a few years before you sell it.

*Me:* But I don't have enough money to buy a big piece of land.

*Dale:* Well, then find someone who has recently

bought a large farm... 160 acres or more, maybe. The new owner won't have any special feelings towards the land, and if he's already farming other land, maybe he won't need the buildings. He might be willing to sell off the barns, along with a few acres.

Dale's ideas got me thinking. How about if I found one or two other people who also wanted to buy a small piece of property? Three of us could pool our resources, buy a sixty-acre parcel, then split it up into thirds. By combining our resources, we could take advantage of the fact that large parcels are easier to find than small ones.

After mentioning the idea to a number of my friends, two of them expressed interest. However, the more we talked about it, the less practical the idea seemed. One of the friends, it turned out, didn't actually have any money to spend, and the other friend said that her ideal piece of property would be located within three or four miles of town. I, of course, didn't want a place that close to civilization.

I finally came to the conclusion that, by looking for a property which suited not only me, but also one or two other persons, the search would actually become *more* difficult.

Before I had a chance to give Dale's ideas any more thought, I got a call from someone about a piece of property that sounded interesting. Very interesting.

## CHAPTER TWENTY-SIX

# EIGHT ACRES ON A CREEK

*Seller:* Eight acres, all timber, real good hunting up there.

The seller had called me on the phone after seeing one of my ads. He wanted $6,400 for the property, which was located in the northeast part of Columbia County.

*Me:* What type of road is it on?

*Seller:* Gravel.

*Me:* How much road frontage is there?

*Seller:* About 310 feet.

*Me:* Is there any water, a well?

*Seller:* Not a well, but rural water runs along the county road. Telephone and electricity are also available.

*Me:* Is the property fenced in?

*Seller:* No.

*Me:* I'd like to look at it. How do I get there?

He gave me directions to the gravel road.

*Seller:* After you've crossed the bridge over the creek, it's two miles up the road on the right.

*Me:* If the property isn't fenced in, how will I know where it is?

*Seller:* You'll see a farmhouse on the left side of the road. My property is opposite that. There's an old post with a metal strap on it. That's where the west end of the property is.

*Me:* How will I know where the east end is?

*Seller:* You'll see an old car by the road. That's where the east boundary is.

*Me:* How far back from the road does the property extend?

*Seller:* All the way down to the creek.

*Me:* Have you ever had it surveyed?

*Seller:* Uh, no.

*Me:* Why are you selling?

*Seller:* We were going to build a house down there, but we've found another parcel closer to town.

*Me:* Have you bought the newer parcel yet?

*Seller:* Uh, no.

The property sounded promising. Eight hundred dollars per acre was the cheapest 8-acre parcel I had come across, and the fact that there was a creek was a real plus.

The property was twenty-two miles from Springfield. Seventeen of those miles were on paved roads, while the remaining miles were over a gravel road that wound its way through hilly, timbered land. As promised, two miles after I crossed the creek I came to a farmhouse on the left. As I parked the car and got out to explore, two dogs ran out from behind the house and started barking.

After walking down the county road, I saw the old car which

marked the eastern boundary of the property. Turning around and heading up the road again, I tried to estimate a distance of 310 feet from the old car.

The ground was thickly overgrown with shrubs and low trees, but back in from the road forty or fifty feet the trees had grown to full height. It was the middle of July, and everything was green.

I noticed that the road was about ten feet higher than the property, with the ground dropping off at a steep angle at the side of the road.

*I could never get my car down this incline. In fact, I'd have to leave the car on the side of the road until I got a driveway put in.*

After a bit of searching, I found the post that the seller had mentioned. It looked as if it had been part of a fence that had run along the side of the road. Nailed to the top of the weather-beaten post was a rusted strap of metal. It brought to mind the descriptions used by pirates to locate buried treasure: "From the rusted metal strap on the post, walk due north 62 feet... "

*OK, this metal strap marks the western boundary. If I head off into the woods from here, I'll have to stay on a course perpendicular to the road.*

Climbing down the incline, I plunged into a cluster of brambles that had sharp thorns. The thorns stuck to my dungarees, and the only way I could extricate myself was to grab hold of each stem, one at a time, and pull them off my pants. I wished that I had brought a pair of heavy gloves.

As soon as I was out of the shrubs and into the taller trees, the walking got easier. The ground foliage wasn't as thick, but I still couldn't walk in a straight line, since there were clumps of trees that I had to walk around. However, since the ground sloped downward, the going was easy. And although it was a hot day, the tree cover protected me from the direct sunlight.

As I got deeper into the woods, it became impossible to know whether I was heading in a straight line. Since I hadn't bothered to note the position of the sun when I was up on the road, I wasn't able to use its position as a guide. My best bet, it seemed, was just to continue going downhill. Eventually, I'd come to the creek.

The incline got steeper, and a number of gullies appeared. Here and there trees had fallen to the ground, and at one point I had to climb over a fallen tree that was about two and a half feet in diameter. I climbed up on the trunk, then jumped down to the ground on the other side.

At the sound of my boots thumping on the ground, a white-spotted fawn leaped out of some foliage not more than eight feet in front of me. It darted off and headed down the hill. The forest was so thick that he was out of sight after he'd run ten feet, but I still got a good look at him.

*I've never been that close to a deer before.*

After about ten minutes of walking, I came to the water. The banks of the creek were about six feet high, and the distance between the banks about thirty feet. However, the width of the flowing water was only ten feet or so.

*What a spot! I could string a hammock between two trees, then lie here and read a book while listening to the gurgling water.*

I took my boots off and waded into the creek. The cold water felt good. There was about a foot of water, more than enough to allow a canoe to navigate.

The water looked fairly clear, but I didn't have any inclination to take a drink of it. Upstream, there were undoubtedly a number of farms. Wastes from farm animals, as well as chemical runoff from fields, probably contaminated the water. However, the creek could still be useful for garden irrigation, washing hands, etc.

I wandered along the creek for awhile, enjoying the beauty of the spot. There was one problem, though. I had no idea where the eastern and western boundaries of the property met the creek. There were no fences, markers, or other indicators of property demarcation.

*This is beautiful land, but since I'm not sure I walked in a straight line coming down here, I don't know whose property I'm on.*

The climb back up to the county road was difficult. Even though the tree cover protected me from the sun, it was a hot afternoon, and soon I was perspiring heavily. It was uphill all the way to the road, and I was winded by the time I got to my car.

Before returning home, though, I decided to visit the courthouse.

\* \* \* \*

At the assessor's office I was told that the taxes on the property were $26 per year. The clerk also told me the book and page number where the deed was recorded.

In the Recorder's Office, where legal documents are kept, I got a photocopy of the deed. The document indicated that when the present owner bought the property two years earlier, he had paid $4.95 in real estate transfer tax. The clerk, after referring to a chart, said that meant the selling price had been approximately $5,000.

The part of the deed which described the property was far from simple. In fact, the document took all of 199 words just to legally delineate the property:

> The Westerly 310 feet (approximately 8 acres more or
> less) of the following described 40 acre tract, to-wit:

Commencing at the Southeast corner of the West Half of the Northwest Quarter (of a specified section, township and range) thence North along the East line of said West Half of the Northwest Quarter of said Section, Township and Range, 746 feet; thence North 68 degrees 37 minutes west, 380 feet; thence North 19 minutes west 442 feet; thence North 54 degrees west, until it strikes the west line of the west half of the Northwest Quarter of said Section; thence South on said West line of said Section to where it intersects the centerline of the public highway, as now located, thence in a Southeasterly direction along the center of said highway, until it strikes the South line of the West Half of the Northwest Quarter of said Section; thence East 596 feet on the South line of said West Half of the Northwest Quarter of said Section to the place of beginning, containing 40 acres, more or less, Columbia County, Iowa. *

Since I couldn't visualize what the property looked like merely by reading the description, I asked the clerk if I could see an aerial photograph of the appropriate township and section.

The clerk, a plump lady in her sixties, brought out a book that was almost four feet long by three feet wide. It must have weighed at least twenty pounds. When we turned to the proper page and located the property, I was surprised at what I saw.

Based on what the seller had told me over the phone, I had assumed that the property's eastern and western boundaries extended perpendicularly from the county road.

---

* The description was a classic example of the "metes and bounds" method of describing property. "Metes" are measurements of length, such as "746 feet." "Bounds" are natural and artificial boundaries, such as "the centerline of the public highway." (The description in a deed can also be based on a reference to a recorded plat or map, or by referring only to township, section, and range.)

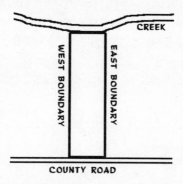

However, there were felt-pen boundary lines on the aerial photo, and they indicated that the property's sides extended away from the road at a sharp angle from the perpendicular.

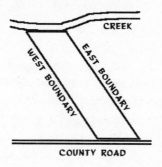

In other words, the property was a parallelogram, but not a rectangle. The references in the deed to angles, and the distances in feet, referred to the large 40-acre tract, which was an irregularly shaped, seven-sided parcel of land. The 8-acre parcel consisted of the westerly 310 feet of the 40-acre parcel.

After purchasing a photocopy of the aerial photo, I sat in my car in the courthouse parking lot and thought about what all this meant.

*The main problem with the property is figuring out where it is.*

*Since there aren't any fences, I'm relying totally on the seller's assurance that the metal strap and the old car mark the boundaries.*

When I got home that night, I called the seller.

> *Me:* How do you know that the western boundary is at the post with the metal strap?
>
> *Seller:* The strap is probably an old marker for the section line, and the deed says the property follows the west line of the section.
>
> *Me:* How do you know the car marks the eastern boundary?
>
> *Seller:* I measured it off from the metal strap.

I held my tongue, but it sounded as if he really didn't know for sure where the boundaries of his property were. His placement of the eastern boundary at the site of the car was dependent on the location of the western boundary, which itself was based on his assumption that the metal strap "probably" marked the section line.

The next day I returned to the courthouse. I wanted to find out whether the assessor would require me to have the property surveyed.

Here's what I learned. In general, a survey is mandated only if the assessor can't determine what the property consists of by reading the legal description in the deed. In that particular county, a distinction is made between "old descriptions" and "new descriptions."

If you are buying a property that is being cut off from a larger parcel (and, therefore, a new description is being drawn up for your property) the rules are stricter. In such a case, your property must be surveyed if the new deed uses the "metes and bounds" method of description. If, however, the new deed bases its description on a reference to section, township, and range, then the property doesn't need to be surveyed.

On the other hand, if you are buying a property that isn't being cut off from a larger parcel (in other words, the seller is transferring to you one hundred percent of the acreage described in the deed that conveyed the property to him) then you don't need a survey, even if your deed uses the metes and bounds method of description. *

For the eight-acre parcel on the creek, the assessor said that their office wouldn't require that the property be surveyed, since the present owner would be conveying one hundred percent of his holding to me. Nevertheless, I asked the assessor for the names of a few surveyors. Even though the county wouldn't require one, it might still be necessary to hire a surveyor so that *I* could figure out where the parcel was located.

That night I called one of the surveyors, and as you'll see in the next chapter, I learned a lot from the conversation.

* The rules vary from county to county as to when surveys are required.

## CHAPTER TWENTY-SEVEN

# LAND SURVEY

*Me:* How much does it cost to have a property surveyed?

*Surveyor:* We charge by the hour, and it will depend on whether there have been other surveys done real close to the property. If there have been, it will be cheaper. Another factor is whether there are section corners* available without having to do a lot of digging and hunting, or researching at the courthouse. The terrain, of course, is another factor, as well as how much foliage there is. And the time of year. It's a lot easier to get around in the woods during the winter than in the summer.

*Me:* Do you have to physically walk around the whole perimeter of the property and count off the feet with a tape measure or chain?

*Surveyor:* We used to have to do that, but we now measure electronically. We get up on a

---

* The majority of the states have been divided into townships and sections. A township is a square area of land containing thirty-six square miles and having sides six miles long. Each township is divided into thirty-six sections. A section is a square area of land containing about 640 acres, with sides approximately one mile long. The sides of a section run north and south. "Section corners" are permanent markers put in the ground by a surveyor at each of the four corners of a section.

high point somewhere and shoot down into the corners. We don't have to actually walk along the line and measure it.

*Me:* Your electronic device tells you the distance?

*Surveyor:* Yup, the distance to the corner. Then we measure an angle to the next corner, and the distance down to it, and then we calculate the distance between the two actual corners.

*Me:* If a property is rectangular, do you sink four markers, one in each corner?

*Surveyor:* Yes.

*Me:* It seems like the biggest factor is whether any other surveys have been done nearby. Does anybody keep a registry that notes where the closest corner markers are?

*Surveyor:* Well, since the 1980s, whenever there is a survey done and there is a division of land, it's required that the surveyor make a plat* and file it at the Recorder's Office at the courthouse. As far as the actual section corners go, records of those would be out at the county engineer's office. But for years, there weren't very good records kept.

*Me:* Will the cost of the survey be affected by the type of description in the deed? For instance, will a metes and bounds description (which makes reference to

---

*A plat is a map made by a surveyor which shows the surveyed property, as well as all survey markers that have been implanted in the ground.

measurements and boundaries) be more difficult for you than a description that refers to township and section?

Surveyor: No, metes and bounds is actually less work, since it indicates that the property has already been surveyed.

Me: I thought some of the old metes and bounds descriptions created problems because they were inexact.

Surveyor: Metes and bounds is the best possible legal description you can have, since it defines the boundaries. If a deed refers to township and section, the first thing you have to do is go out and establish where that section is. Then you have to divide the section into quarters, then divide the quarter into halves, and so forth. By the time you do that, you may find fence lines out there that don't agree with where the actual divisions are, and then you've got conflicts. A reference to township and section may not define very well where the actual boundaries are.

Me: What are your fees like?

Surveyor: We charge $55 an hour for the two-man crew. Time in the courthouse is $30 an hour, and our drafting time on the computer is $25 an hour. How many acres is this parcel?

Me: Eight.

Surveyor: Is it in rough ground?

Me: Sort of rough. All timber.

*Surveyor:* I'm kinda shooting from the hip, but I'd
think you could get in for anywhere from
$900 to $1,000. I'd be real surprised if it
would get over $1,200 to $1,400.

\* \* \* \*

Realizing that I would save a lot of money if I could survey the
property myself, I took another look at the photocopy of the
aerial photograph. According to the photograph's felt-pen
markings (which outlined the property lines of all the parcels
shown on the photograph) the eastern boundary line for the
property across the road (the property with the farmhouse on it)
met the road at a point approximately half way between the
western and eastern boundary lines of the 8-acre parcel.

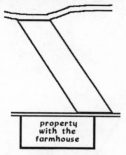

If I could pinpoint on the ground the location of the eastern
boundary line for the farmhouse property, maybe I could use
that as a starting point to mark off the boundaries of the 8-acre
parcel. I realized, of course, that such a "do-it-yourself" survey
couldn't determine the precise boundaries, nor would it have any
legal effect. However, if my own survey gave a fair
approximation of the boundaries, maybe that would be good
enough for my own purposes.

The next weekend, after returning to the property, I walked
across the road and knocked on the door of the farmhouse. A

man in his forties, bare-chested and as big as Paul Bunyan, came to the door.

I told him that I was thinking about buying the property across the road, but that I was trying to figure out where the property actually was. He came out to the road with me, along with a teenage boy and two dogs, and pointed out his western boundary line.

"If you buy the place and need any help," he said, "just holler."

\* \* \* \*

The next step was to see if I could determine how much road frontage the 8-acre parcel had. This measurement wasn't specified in the deed, since the document merely described the property by referring to "the westerly 310 feet" of the larger, 40-acre tract. Moreover, this 310-foot figure did *not* refer to one of the boundary lines of the 8-acre parcel (as the seller had suggested) but rather, represented the height of the parallelogram which was formed by the property's boundaries.

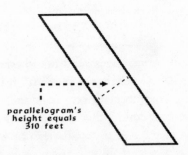

parallelogram's
height equals
310 feet

Holding a metric ruler over the photo, I noted that the parallelogram's height measured 22 centimeters on the ruler. Then, after repositioning the ruler so it was on top of the road, I measured that distance, which turned out to be 27 centimeters.

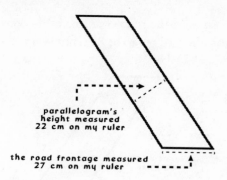

parallelogram's
height measured
22 cm on my ruler

the road frontage measured
27 cm on my ruler

Next, I used an equation based on a principle I learned in my ninth grade algebra class:

$$\frac{22}{310} = \frac{27}{x}$$

$$22\ x\ =\ 310 \times 27$$

$$22\ x\ =\ 8{,}370$$

$$x\ =\ 380.45\ \text{feet}$$

According to my calculation, there were about 380 feet of road frontage. Of course, this figure was only an approximation, since it was based on my rough measurements of the felt-pen markings on the photograph.

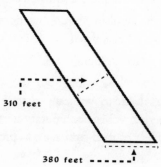

310 feet

380 feet

143

Next, I positioned the ruler over one of the long sides of the property, which turned out to be 85 centimeters.

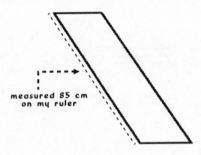

measured 85 cm
on my ruler

Then, using the same algebraic formula, I calculated the length of the property:

$$\frac{22}{310} = \frac{85}{x}$$

$$22\,x = 310 \times 85$$

$$22\,x = 26{,}350$$

$$x = 1{,}197.72 \ \text{feet}$$

By miltiplying the length of the property by its height, I could determine the parcel's square footage:

1,197.72x310 feet = 371,293.2 square feet

Then, dividing the resulting figure by the number of square feet in an acre (43,560), I calculated the size of the parcel in acres:

371,293.2 square feet / 43,560 = 8.523719 acres

This 8.5-figure was close enough to the "8 acres more or less"noted in the deed to indicate that I was doing my calculations properly. My computation that there were approximately 380 feet of road frontage was probably not too far off.

Now that I had a figure for the amount of road frontage, I felt confident that, if I bought the property, I could conduct my own rough survey and mark out the boundaries.

All I would have to do, I reasoned, would be to start at the spot where the farmhouse owner said his property line was. If I crossed the road to the 8-acre parcel, I'd be at the midpoint of the southern side of my property. Then, using a tape measure, I could start walking east along the road. When I had gone approximately 190 feet (half the width of the property) I'd be at the eastern boundary of my property. Then, after returning to the midpoint of the property, I'd walk west for 190 feet to locate the western boundary.

To find the direction of the western side of the property, I had only to look to the deed. The document described that line with the words, "thence south on said west line of" the section "to where it intersects the center-line of the public highway..."

Since section lines run exactly north and south, all I'd have to do would be to start at the road and head directly north. To accomplish that, I could rent or borrow a surveyor's transit and plot out the property's western boundary. I felt confident that, if I bought the property, I could perform a rough survey by myself.

The big question was, did I want to buy the property? And before I could answer that, there were a couple of important things that I needed to find out.

## Chapter Twenty-Eight

# THE COST OF UTILITIES

I was curious to find out how much it would cost to bring rural water onto the property. Although I probably wouldn't need running water for myself, especially since there was water in the creek year-round, I was still interested in how much the rural water hookup would cost. If I ever wanted to sell the property, the cost of good drinking water would likely be a main concern to potential buyers.

When I called the rural water department I was told that their water main extended to the farmhouse, but didn't go any further down the road. The farmer had paid $3,000 four years earlier to bring the line down the road to his farm.

If I wanted to tap into the line, I'd have to pay two separate fees. The first fee would be $1,000, which the water company would turn over to the farmer as a kind of reimbursement, since he had paid such a large sum to extend the main down to his property (and thus, also down to the 8-acre property).

However, I'd have to pay the $1,000 reimbursement fee only if I went ahead with the water installation sometime within the next twelve months. If, on the other hand, I waited a year before having the hookup done, I wouldn't have to pay the reimbursement fee. (The company's rules specified that all future customers who tied into an extension within five years were required to partially reimburse the customer who had originally paid for the extension.)

The second fee that I'd incur would cover the cost of extending the line from in front of the farmhouse, under the road, to the 8-acre parcel, and for the installation of a meter. That fee would be approximately $1,100. From then on, the minimum monthly charge would be $18.72. This would give me 2,000 gallons per month.

Because I had seen a telephone pedestal beside the road in front of the farmhouse, I knew that a telephone line ran along the county road.*

I called the telephone company and found out that, in addition to the regular hook-up fees, a new rural residential installation would cost 72 cents for every foot that the line had to run from the pedestal.

I estimated that the pedestal was about 110 feet from the 8-acre parcel. That meant it would cost about $79 just to extend the cable to the property line. How much more it would cost would depend on how far into the property I wanted the phone to be located. Although I had no plans to install a phone, I had found out that the cost, at least, wouldn't be prohibitive.

\* \* \* \*

I visited the property again. As I fought my way through the trees down towards the creek, I tried to picture what I would do with the property if I bought it.

*First, I'd have to buy a chain saw and cut some of the trees down.*

The whole property was wooded, which meant that no part of it would thoroughly dry out, especially during the rainy season. I'd want at least one clearing so there'd be a spot that the sun would get to.

---

* A telephone pedestal is a metal post which sticks out of the ground about three feet. It contains a junction box allowing easy hook-up to an underground telephone cable just below the surface of the ground.

*Next, I'd have to put in an access driveway and construct a barn or garage.*

A building would be necessary to store the tractor. I didn't want to leave it out in the open where it would accumulate any more rust than it already had. But more importantly, I didn't want somebody to be able to come along and steal parts off the tractor.

It took me about seven minutes of bushwhacking to reach the creek. On my previous visits to the property, the water had been flowing slowly and its level had been low.

This time, though, the water was making so much noise that I heard it about 150 feet away. When I got to the water's edge, it looked more like a river than a creek. The watercourse filled the 30-foot channel and came up almost to the tops of the banks. I estimated the depth of water to be at least five feet.

The water was flowing past so quickly that I doubted it would be possible to swim in it. The speed of the water, as well as its noise, excited me.

*This is beautiful. If I had a cabin down here by the creek's edge, I could lie in bed at night and listen to the roar of the water.*

After returning to my car, I wrote down on a piece of paper the property's good and bad features:

> Good Features
> on a creek
> lots of timber
> not too far from Springfield
> rural water, electricity and telephone available
> on gravel road
> not too much traffic
> $6,400 price is within my budget
> farmer across road very friendly
> property is on hill (not boring flat land)

<u>Bad Features</u>
have to conduct own survey (or hire surveyor)
no access driveway
not particularly isolated (farmhouse across road)

The good features clearly outnumbered the bad, and I decided to make an offer on the property. However, I was still faced with a difficult question: how much should I offer?

## Chapter Twenty-Nine

# HOW LOW
# SHOULD MY OFFER BE

I decided to get some advice from Steve, an acquaintance of mine who had bought and sold real estate back East.

*Me:* I'm ready to make an offer on a property I've found, but I don't know how low an offer to make.

*Steve:* How much is he asking?

*Me:* Six thousand four hundred.

*Steve:* Offer him three thousand.

*Me:* Umm... isn't that too low?

*Steve:* No. Once you make your offer, you can't negotiate the price down any further. It can only go up. Anyway, sixty-four hundred is merely his asking price. He *expects* you to counter with a low offer.

*Me:* Maybe you're right, since I won't ask for installment payments. I'm going to pay cash.

*Steve:* Ok, here's what to do. Go to the bank and get $3,000 in five-dollar bills. Put all the money in a suitcase. Then go to the seller. Set the suitcase down on his kitchen table and open the lid. Let me tell ya, Ralph, there's something about the sight of hard cash.... it's a real persuader.

Me: But I was going to go to an attorney and have him draw up the offer in writing.

Steve: Why do you need an attorney? Believe me, lawyers have screwed up more real estate deals than you could ever imagine. I had a big sale just on the verge of going through, then the buyer gets an attorney. All of a sudden, a whole bunch of objections are raised and the deal gets killed.

There was no way that I was going to shove a suitcase full of $3,000 into the seller's face, so I decided to talk to Diane, my friend who had been a real estate agent.

Me: I've found a property I want, but I don't know whether to make the offer in writing, or verbally. There's no real estate agent involved.

Diane: Do it in writing. Any agreement you reach that's not in writing has no effect. It can't be enforced.

Me: How about if I make the initial offer verbally, just to see what he'll say. That will be a lot easier than having to draw up a formal offer.

Diane: You *can* do it verbally, but the problem is, when you later go to write it down, you and the seller may remember what you've agreed upon slightly differently. Maybe he'll say, "I wanted such-and-such down," but you remember a different amount.

There are so many little details that are essential to the offer, it's hard to nail them all down in a conversation. What happens is, later on, if you haven't agreed on every one of the details, all you've got is an agreement to agree, which is not a contract.

*Me:* If the offer's got to be in writing, does that mean I should *never* talk to him about price?

*Diane:* Go ahead and make a verbal offer if you want, but reduce it to writing as soon as possible. Immediately reduce it to writing.

*Me:* Ok, let's say I'm making my offer. Maybe it's in writing, or maybe verbally. Is it good psychology for me to point out the things I don't like about the property?

*Diane:* You can certainly mention difficulties about the property, but you bring those things up when you're looking at the land with the seller. You might say, "Oh, there's no road here," or, "I really wanted a place with a view." After the discussions, then you make the offer in writing.

*Me:* I'm thinking about making a real, real low offer.

*Diane:* Sometimes a low-ball offer can make a seller so angry that he'll refuse to have anything further to do with you. Especially when you're dealing with farmers who don't really need or want to sell, necessarily.

*Me:* I think this guy really wants to sell.

Diane: He can still get mad as hell at you, especially when you're making the offer yourself, without an agent as the middleman.

Me: It seems like I've read about lots of buyers making low-ball offers.

Diane: Sure, but a low-ball can poison the negotiation early on. It's like asking a woman out in a very crude manner. If your first approach to a woman is crude and offensive, you may never get a date with her.

Me: I don't doubt that a low-ball can ruin *some* deals, but...

Diane: Often, the seller's identity and self respect are identified with his property. Real property is something that's very dear to people. The property may have been in the family for generations, and if you make a low-ball offer, it's kind of like kicking one of his kids, or saying, "What a mangy looking dog you have."

Although what she was saying made sense, I was enjoying playing devil's advocate so much that it was hard to stop arguing.

Me: This property hasn't been in his family for generations.

Diane: It doesn't matter. You don't want to say something that will make him mad. Low-balling is a highly risky tactic.

Me: It's *never* a smart thing to do?

Diane: It may be ok for buyers who are looking

for investment properties. People who low-ball are basically just trolling for somebody who's desperate. And when they find that desperate person, they make the killer deal. Then they put that trophy up on their wall and boast to their friends, "I stole this property."

*Me:* I'm not doing this for an investment. But still, maybe I'm willing to gamble that he...

*Diane:* My experience was, over and over, if you make a deal (even if it's in writing) and the other person later on says to himself, "I got shafted, this is not a deal that is good for me," he'll find a way to get out of it. The deal will fall through, it won't happen. Or maybe it will go through, but when you end up with the property, you'll find that the guy took all the fixtures, or cut all the trees down, or did something vindictive. Maybe you bought the house because of this beautiful old oak tree in the back, and guess what? When you get the property, he's cut the tree into lumber. You have to sue him for it, but it won't do any good because even a court judgment can't replace that oak tree.

*Me:* So how much *should* I offer him? I've read where you're never supposed to offer more than seventy-five per cent of the seller's asking price.

*Diane:* Anybody who uses a formula like that is just deluding himself. He's trying to make life simpler than it is. There are no perfect formulas for determining the amount of a buyer's offer, just like there are no perfect formulas for determining the seller's asking price. How do you think the seller came up with his price?

*Me:* Maybe he had the property appraised.

*Diane:* Appraisals, evaluations, comparisons... those are all just big guesses. What it comes down to is, somebody just made up the asking price. Completely out of the blue, possibly.

*Me:* Boy, you're not much help.

*Diane:* Every piece of real estate is unique, and the buyer's and seller's needs are unique. A real estate purchase is one of the few unique transactions that take place in America. In our culture, almost everything else we do is all fixed for us. We go into Wal-Mart and there's the price. But when purchasing real estate, the bargaining is potentially infinite. Not only can you argue about the price, you can also argue about the terms. Consider this: I'll pay you any price you want for a piece of property, provided I can dictate the terms. You name the price.

*Me:* Any price at all?

*Diane:* Sure. I'll pay you a million dollars for a dinky little piece of property if I can give you a penny down, then a dollar a year until it's paid off.

A mischievous little grin appeared on her face, and I then asked her if I needed an attorney to draw up my offer.

*Diane:* Unless you're very experienced, unless you've bought a lot of properties, you probably will need some professional help. An attorney or a real estate broker. They'll make sure that all the paperwork is done correctly. If you're not experienced in that, you could miss a piece of paper here or there that could get you in big trouble.

*Me:* I've definitely decided that I want my own attorney to be with me at the closing. I might as well have him involved right from the beginning, and have him draw up the offer.

*Diane:* Attorneys may not be so good in the negotiation process. That's not where their expertise is, unless they've bought and sold a great deal of real estate. Where an attorney can be useful is by asking, "Let me see now, how many possible ways can this transaction go wrong? Let's write down on paper what we're going to do if those things happen." But when it comes to what you should offer and what you shouldn't, and the style of making the offer in your area, that's where a real estate broker can be useful.

*Me:* But if my attorney draws up an offer that's specifically tailored for me, won't that protect my interests more than the broker's standard form?

*Diane:* No, not usually. In fact, it's usually best to use the broker's form because that's the one that people are most likely to have seen. The broker's standard forms are like dollar bills, in a sense. Everybody recognizes them and accepts them. All you have to do is fill in the blanks, like how much is the price, and what are the terms. A standard form is less likely to spook the seller. If your attorney has drawn up a special document for you, the seller might even have to ask his own attorney about how your offer compares with the usual language in the standard real estate contract.

*Me:* I've got one last question, but I don't know... maybe the question indicates that I'm really not ready to buy. To be honest, I have some reservations about purchasing this property, but I'm afraid that if I *don't* buy it, nothing better will come along.

*Diane:* There will always be other properties. Who knows, you might like the next property even better. On the other hand, maybe this property *is* the one for you.

*Me:* But I have this fear in my gut...

*Diane:* That's a standard emotion. Besides, there are so many things that can go wrong when you're buying property. If this property isn't meant for you for some reason, there will be plenty of ways for the powers of the universe to block the sale.

*Me:* Is that a belief from some California mystical philosophy?

*Diane:* Maybe. But if it isn't your destiny to have that property, you probably won't end up with it.

\* \* \* \*

I finally decided that, if I was going to make an offer, I'd have an attorney draw it up for me. I was still hesitant, though, about the whole transaction. Did I really want this property? In order to help me make up my mind, I decided to visit the place one more time.

When I pulled up in front of the property, the first thing I saw was a metal sign. A real estate sign had been driven into the ground right next to the road. I wrote down the telephone number of the broker, then hiked down to the creek.

The water had subsided since my last visit, but the spot was still beautiful. As I stood next to the water's edge under the shade of a large tree, a cool breeze blew across the water and brushed my face. Something inside me said, "Go ahead and buy it."

As soon as I got home, I telephoned the broker to see if the price was still $6,400. It was. Next, I went to an attorney and asked about his fees. His standard fee, he said, for handling a real estate transaction, including everything from the offer through the closing, was $200. However, if the offer turned out not to be accepted, he'd charge only $25 for having drawn it up. I handed him a photocopy of the deed that I'd gotten at the courthouse, since he needed to know the legal description of the property. I would offer $5,000, with $375 as a deposit.

The next day I drove over to the broker's office and handed him the offer, along with a check for $375. The transaction, which took less than two minutes, seemed sort of anticlimactic. As I left the office, I felt almost relieved, but I also felt a little scared. Although I no longer had to be concerned about how much to offer, I was still worrying about whether this was the right property.

As fate would have it, an unexpected telephone call was going to answer that question for me.

CHAPTER THIRTY

# AN UNEXPECTED BARN

When I got home that night at five in the evening there was a message on my answering machine:

> *Seller:* Ah... yes... my name is Thomas Waterhouse. I saw your ad* and I got some property down here near Union Springs, in Fillmore County. Fifteen acres. My number is... my number is... oh ... my number... Hey, Bernice, what's our telephone number? ...my number is 555–2585. Good by.

Union Springs is a small town about sixteen miles from Springfield, well within my 25-mile target area. Even though I had submitted an offer on the 8-acre property earlier that day, it hadn't, as far as I knew, been accepted. I was curious about this latest call, since fifteen acres was just the right size. I immediately telephoned the seller.

> *Me:* Can you tell me something about the property?
>
> *Seller:* It's mostly timber. There was a mobile

---

* He responded to an advertisement I had run for three consecutive weeks in one of the weekly newspapers in Fillmore County. The ad was identical to the one I described in Chapter Twelve. He told me later that, although he saw the ad the first week it appeared, it wasn't until he saw it the second time that he decided to call me.

home, but that's been taken off.

*Me:* How much do you want for it?

*Seller:* Six thousand.

My heart started to beat faster. What if this property was nicer than the 8-acre parcel?

*Me:* What kind of a road is it on?

*Seller:* Gravel.

*Me:* Do you know if there is a rural water line
    on that road?

*Seller:* Yes, there is. It's never been brought in,
    though. But there's a cabin down in the
    woods.

An image appeared in my mind of a small log cabin nestled in the woods, with smoke coming out of a stone chimney.

I was so excited that I decided to visit the place immediately. Using the directions the seller gave me, I looked at my plat map and plotted the shortest route to the property.

During the drive down, I found that three-quarters of the distance was on paved, county roads. As I followed the route south, I ran into little traffic. The last few miles were over gravel roads that ran through rolling countryside. That part of the county was a mixture of crop, pasture, and timber.

The gravel road wound back-and-forth, following the course of the Black Creek. The road crossed the creek over a narrow concrete bridge, then started up a steep hill. The property stood at the top of the hill, at a spot where the road made a sharp curve. My first glimpse of the setting startled me.

*Oh, my God. This is wonderful. Look at those trees.*

The land was covered with 50-foot trees. Most were tall oaks, but interspersed here and there were a few evergreens. On the opposite side of the gravel road, on property that someone else owned, horses were grazing on hilly pasture-land.

*I can't believe it! It's so beautiful.*

The spot was isolated. I had passed the closest neighbor a quarter of a mile down the road, but even that cluster of farm buildings couldn't be seen from the Waterhouse property because of a grove of trees.

There was an access road onto the property, but instead of pulling into it, I parked my car on the shoulder of the county road. I wanted to walk onto the property, not drive onto it. The setting was so beautiful that I already felt a degree of reverence towards it.

The sun was setting, and its red glow cast onto the trees a strange but beautiful tint. As I walked down the property's dirt road, I became aware of my breathing. I stopped walking, stood up straight, and inhaled deeply.

*This air sure smells good.*

About seventy-five feet into the property, the dirt road split into two roads. One headed down a slight slope, deeper into the property. I took the other road, which turned left and headed north.

This road had been cut through the woods and was just wide enough for one vehicle. Tree branches on both sides of the road formed a canopy over the road, and with the heavy foliage on the trees, it was as if I were walking through a tunnel.

The road surface was covered with fallen leaves, and as my shoes crunched the leaves underneath, I could feel the contours of the wheel ruts in the ground. Wagon or tractor tires had probably rolled over this road for years. The two tracks where wheels had traveled had sunk a good four inches into the ground, leaving a hump in the middle.

The lane didn't run in a straight line, but zig-zagged back and forth, following the course of the land and avoiding big trees.

After I had walked about 500 feet, I came to an open spot. The clearing was covered with brown grass about two feet tall. At the north side of the clearing was a barbed wire fence. I looked out over the fence.

*What a view!*

Beyond the fence, the land fell off gently. In front of me was a panorama of the valley below. I could just barely see two farms in the distance, and at the other side of the valley, about two miles away, the hills rose.

*What a great spot for a cabin. I'd be able to wake up in the morning and look out over the valley. And there's already a road in here.*

It was getting late, and I wanted to explore the other branch of the road while there was still light. As I walked back up the zig-zag road, I noticed an electric utility pole that I hadn't seen when I first passed the spot.

*This must be where the mobile home was.*

As I walked back to where the road had split, I remembered that I had just made an offer on the 8-acre parcel.

*Although the 8-acre property is pretty in some ways, it has no roads on it. But here, the road's already built.*

When I reached the split in the road, I turned left and started down the other lane. It, too, meandered through the woods, but it was on land that sloped downward gently.

About 500 feet in from the county road, I saw a building. It was a one-story barn, about thirty by sixty feet in size.

*There's a barn, plus a cabin? This is just too good to be true.*

At one end of the building was a large opening, roughly twelve feet wide by seven feet high. It was pitch black inside, and I stepped inside cautiously, not wanting to fall down if there was a hole in the ground.

I walked around the inside of the barn gingerly, worrying that I'd bump into something. The barn turned out to be empty, though. I noticed, too, that there weren't any posts in the middle of the building. The inside was one large room. After a few minutes, my eyes adjusted to the darkness, and I was able to see how the barn was constructed.

It was a pole building, with 8x8-inch posts sunk into the ground every six feet around the perimeter. There was a gable roof that was supported by trusses. The floor was dirt, and the building had five windows.

*This is huge. I bet there's room in here for six tractors.*

Daylight was almost gone, but I still wanted to find the cabin. As I continued down the dirt road, which led further into the woods, I heard the chirping of crickets. When I got closer to them, their chirping stopped. When I passed, the sound resumed.

The road continued beyond the barn about 400 feet, then opened up into a large clearing. As I stood in the center of the opening, I realized I was in the middle of a dark forest. Except for the moon and stars above, I was surrounded by blackness. I stood motionless and quiet. The chirping of crickets seemed louder, and a slight breeze rustled the leaves in the trees.

*What a peaceful, isolated, spot.*

But where was the cabin? I wanted to continue exploring, but decided to get back to the car before I got lost in the dark.

During the drive back home I realized that *this* was the property that I wanted. But what, I wondered, should I do about my offer on the 8-acre parcel?

## CHAPTER THIRTY-ONE

# THE LAST EXPLORATION

If it wasn't too late, I had to revoke my offer on the 8-acre property.

Early the next morning I called the real estate agent. As I dialed his number, I realized I was nervous. I had the same feeling of discomfort I've had when I've had to tell an employer I was quitting a job.

> *Me:* Has the seller had a chance to consider my offer?
>
> *Agent:* We haven't been able to reach him. He must be out of town.
>
> *Me:* You may not believe this, but I got a call from another seller last night, and he has fifteen acres that suit my needs even more. I want to revoke my offer on the 8-acre property.

I was afraid that the agent would think I had gotten cold feet, and that, as an excuse to revoke the offer, I was making up the story about a new piece of property.

> *Agent:* Can I ask the location of it? I'm just curious.
>
> *Me:* It's in Rockland Township.
>
> *Agent:* Way up by Union Springs... south of Locust Valley?

His questioning worried me. What if he found out where the Waterhouse property was, then offered the seller more than $6,000?

> *Me:* Um... west of Woodbridge.
>
> *Agent:* I didn't know there were any 15-acre parcels for sale up there. How far are you from the blacktop? I hope you don't think I'm being nosy.
>
> *Me:* Tell you what. Once it gets finalized, I'll let you know where it is.
>
> *Agent:* OK, sure. I mean, I was trying... I'm just glad you found it. I'm amazed that you... small acreages are so hard to come by.
>
> *Me:* What do we do now? Can I stop by and pick up my offer?
>
> *Agent:* Whatever. We always mark "void" on the check whenever it's no deal. I'd rather that you get something you really want. No problem.

What a relief. If my offer had already been accepted, I would have had to try to buy my way out of the contract. Now I was free to pursue the Waterhouse property.*

Next, I called Mr. Waterhouse.

> *Me:* I went down and saw the property last night, and I really like it. I'm going to visit the place again this morning. I want to walk around the whole fence line.
>
> *Seller:* You'll build up quite a sweat, 'cause there's some pretty steep ground back in there.

---

* I picked up the offer and the check the next day from the agent, who didn't seem particularly fazed by my revocation.

*Me:* By the way. I saw the barn, but I couldn't find the cabin.

*Seller:* Oh, the barn... That's what I meant by "cabin." We were going to turn the barn into a cabin.

Although it was a weekday, I took the day off to make the trip to the property. I wanted to visit the place during daylight, before I made a final decision whether to buy it.

I arrived at the property around 10 A.M. The sun was bright, and it was already warm. It was going to be a hot day.

This time, I drove the car onto the property and wound my way over the dirt road to the barn. As soon as I turned the car's engine off, I felt the peacefulness of the property's quiet setting. I sat in the car for a few minutes, doing nothing. Then I got out and walked around the barn.

*Gosh, this building is just perfect. It looks like it's in pretty good condition, too.*

I wasn't particularly disappointed that there was no cabin, since a barn would be more useful. My immediate need was for a place to shelter the tractor, and I could always add a cabin later on.

Deciding to inspect the fences before it got too hot, I walked back up to the front of the property. I noticed that there had been, at one time, a barbed wire fence which had run along the county road. The fence posts had rotted out, however, and the wire had fallen over to the ground.

There were standing fences, though, on the north and south sides of the property. I started walking along the north fence line.

Mr. Waterhouse had been right. The fence traversed a number of deep gullies, some almost sixty feet deep. As I climbed up and down each gully, I noted the condition of the fence to see if there were any breaks that would need repairing. I knew that, under Iowa law, if a neighbor relied on one of the fences to confine cattle on his land, I would be held responsible for the upkeep of half the length of the fence.

After the fourth gully, I was winded. I took off my shirt and sat down on the ground. The sun was shining brightly, but from my spot on the forest floor, I was protected from the sun's glare. It was dark and cool under the trees.

After a few more minutes of climbing and walking, the fence I was following intersected another fence that ran north and south. I followed this new fence south down into another gully. At the bottom of the gully was a dry stream bed.

I continued to follow this fence, which marked the back side of the property, until I came to another intersection of fences. I was now at the southeast corner of the property. Needing another rest, I sat down and leaned against the trunk of a huge tree.

About thirty feet below me, where two other small streams converged, I could hear the water rippling over the rocks. I sat under the tree for about ten minutes, thinking about what it would be like to own the property. Then, very slowly, I began to realize how comfortable I felt.

*Wow. This spot is so isolated, nobody could ever bother me here. Even if there was somebody on the property, they would never climb up and down the gullies to get here. At this spot, nobody could ever see me, or hear me.*

After a few more minutes, I realized I didn't hear any unnatural sounds. No cars. No lawn mowers. No doors slamming.

But there were sounds. I heard a bird chirping. It must have been close, but I couldn't see it. Then I heard another bird, one with a different kind of chirp. This bird was perched on the branch of a low bush next to one of the streams. I whistled at it, trying to mimic its call.

After awhile, I heard raindrops. At first, there was only an occasional plop-plop. Then the rain picked up, and the sound was like gentle drum beats on the leaves. Then it started to rain hard, but because the foliage overhead was so dense, I wasn't getting wet.

Then I heard the wind. It picked up quickly, and soon it was so strong that I could no longer hear the rain drops, even though I could now feel them falling on my head.

All of a sudden there was a big gush of wind and a clap of thunder.

*Hey, that's not thunder.*

When a second thundering boom occurred, I realized that the noise was caused by two trees scraping together. The sound was so sharp and loud that it sounded just like thunder. Then I heard other trees making similar noises, except they were scraping together more slowly. They sounded like creaking doors – very loud creaking doors.

*This property is beautiful. I really should buy it.*

After the storm subsided, I got up and walked along the south fence line. It, too, went up and down a number of gulches. After a few minutes, I arrived back at the county road. I had walked around the perimeter of the property.*

I now had a fairly good idea of the shape of the property. The west side of the parcel abutted the county road, which made a curve at that spot. The three other sides of the property – north, east, and south – were delineated by fences. At both the northeast corner and the southeast corner, the fences met at

---

* Months later I calculated the distance around the property to be approximately six tenths of a mile.

right angles. Thus, the property was roughly rectangular.

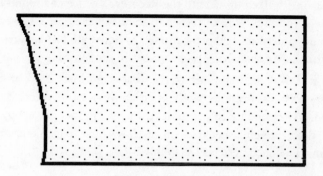

Next, I decided to see what I could find out at the courthouse in Warrensburg. When I entered the tax assessor's office, I worried about what kind of reception I would receive. I had inquired about so many pieces of property during the past months that it wouldn't have surprised me if the courthouse employees thought of me as a pest. However, they were as pleasant as ever.

> *Me:* Just one last piece of property. Can you tell me what the taxes are on this 15-acre parcel?

I pointed the parcel out to her on my plat map, and she looked the records up on a computer.

> *Assessor:* Twenty dollars, due in two installments.

> *Me:* Forty dollars a year?

> *Assessor:* No. Ten dollars each installment. Total of twenty dollars each year.

> *Me:* If I bought the property, would you require that I have it surveyed?

> *Assessor:* If the parcel's not being divided up, no.

After getting the book and page number for the deed from the assessor, I walked upstairs to the Recorder's office and found the proper volume. When I turned to the designated page, however, I found a deed to a different property. Someone had apparently written down the wrong page number in the records.

I had to make a number of trips back and forth between the Assessor's and Recorder's offices before I was able to locate the deed. After finding the document, I paid 25 cents for a copy of the deed, which was typed on an Iowa State Bar Association form. The document read as follows:

### WARRANTY DEED

For the consideration of Four Hundred Fifty and no/100 Dollars ($450.00) and other valuable consideration* Stanley M. Bowman and Ruth W. Hughes, husband and wife, do hereby Convey to Thomas W. Waterhouse and Bernice A. Waterhouse, husband and wife, the following described real estate in Fillmore County, Iowa:

Fifteen (15) acres lying east of the public highway in the North Half of the Southwest Quarter (SW1/4) of the Southeast Quarter (SE1/4) in (a specified section, township, and range) in Fillmore County, IA.

Consideration less than $500.00

Grantors do Hereby Covenant with grantees, and successors in interest, that grantors hold the real estate by title in fee simple; that they have good and lawful authority to sell and convey the real estate; that the real estate is Free and Clear of all Liens and Encumbrances except as may be above stated; and grantors Covenant to

* I was told that the Waterhouses acquired the land for $450 plus satisfaction of a loan owed them by the sellers. Since I didn't know the amount of the loan, I couldn't determine how much the Waterhouses had paid for the property.

Warrant and Defend the real estate against the lawful claims of all persons except as may be above stated. Each of the undersigned hereby relinquishes all rights of dower, homestead and distributive share in and to the real estate.

Dated: 2/22/89          (Signed by grantors)

I then asked to see an aerial photograph of the property. The clerk laid out on the counter one of the huge, twenty-by-forty-inch, black and white photographs. The boundaries of each parcel were highlighted with felt-pen lines, but when I spotted the Waterhouse property, I was shocked.

The boundary markings on the aerial photo indicated that the southern boundary of the property was zig-zagged, rather than straight. In other words, the property was quite irregular in shape:

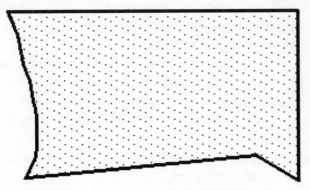

*Me:* Who drew in the boundary lines?

*Recorder:* The soil team.

*Me:* When was that done?

*Recorder:* Years ago.

*Me:* What did they use to determine these lines?

*Recorder:* I don't know.

This was troubling. The southern boundary marking on the photo didn't jibe with the southern fence line, which from my observation, appeared to run in a straight line from west to east.

The deed, which wasn't specific enough to clear up the discrepancy, described the property only as, "Fifteen acres lying east of the public highway in the North Half of the Southwest Quarter... "

I called my attorney as soon as I got home. He reassured me that it was the *deed* which determined the boundaries of the property, not a diagram made by a soil team member. He admitted that the deed's "Fifteen acres lying east of the public highway" seemed "a bit vague." He said, however, that if that was the legal description which had been used in a number of transfers over the years, and if it was fairly easy to determine the boundaries from a physical inspection of the property, and if the county assessor was comfortable with the deed's description, then I shouldn't worry about it.

When I asked him what would happen if it turned out that the fences were really in the wrong place, he had a reassuring answer for that, too. If the fences had been there for ten or more years, he said, then the fences would have become the legal property line.

After returning to Springfield, I called up the surveyor I had talked to a few weeks earlier.

> *Me:* What if, after you conduct a survey, you find out that the boundaries you laid down differ from an existing fence line?
>
> *Surveyor:* That's a good question. We'd have to examine the fence lines, examine the deed and the chain of title, and find out, first of all, why there is a difference; why there is a conflict. And sometimes it could be easily

explained. Maybe the fence was put in for convenience sake. In other words, intentionally not put on the line. Or maybe it was unintentional, and it's always been accepted as the line. And sometimes an incorrect fence line can become the legal line.

*Me:* You mean after ten years?

*Surveyor:* Yes, sometimes, but not always. Lot of people say, "Oh yeah, a fence line becomes the actual boundary line after ten years." But that's not always the case. I wish it was that cut and dry. Adverse possession and acquiescence is a real involved and complicated subject. We study court cases on this a lot. It seems like almost every case is different: how the fence was put in, when the fence was put in, and by whom. There's lots of evidence to gather.

After hanging up the phone and thinking about the whole thing for a few minutes, I realized I was making too much out of the question of the fences. Since my attorney had reassured me that I didn't have to worry about it, why didn't I just accept that?

There was, however, one last thing that I wanted to find out about the property, and that was what it would cost to have rural water connected.

I had to call a number of different rural water companies before I found the one that serviced that part of the county. My call was transferred to Frank, a customer service representative who had in front of him an aerial photo of the appropriate portion of the township. He could actually see on the photo, he said, the road that led into the woods to the barn on the 15-acre parcel.

> *Frank:* Our main line goes all the way up and down that county road. We're on the west side, on the other side of the road from you. Just looking at it, I'd say it's going to cost you right around $1,000 to have us come across the road and set a meter pit. It looks like your property is going to need a pressure regulator, too.
>
> *Me:* Why is that?
>
> *Frank:* We try to use seventy pounds as a cut off.
>
> *Me:* You mean that if the pressure's too high in the main, you need a regulator?
>
> *Frank:* Right. So it's going to come up to right around $1,000. Unless, of course, there's a reverse easement on the property.
>
> *Me:* What's that?
>
> *Frank:* Well, when we first bring our main down a road, we request an easement from each property owner along the way. Most people grant the easement. But once in a while, somebody doesn't give permission. Then there's a reverse easement on their property.
>
> *Me:* So what happens? What's the result?
>
> *Frank:* Well, if the owner of that property later decides that he wants to hook up to the system, he has to pay a reverse easement fee.
>
> *Me:* How much is that?

*Frank:* It depends. It's a dollar a foot for everything we had to lay in the ditch, or everything we had to move to the other side of the road, but there's a $500 minimum. Let's say you only own an acre. If you wouldn't give easement at the time, and we had to lay out, say, 100 feet, you'd still have the $500 minimum fee. But I'm checking my records here, and I don't find a reverse easement for that property.

*Me:* Once you get hooked up, what's the minimum charge per month?

*Frank:* Minimum is $18.90. That gives you 2,000 gallons, but a family's not going to be able to get by with the minimum, unless you're awful conservative. The average family of four or five is going to use 4,000 to 5,000 gallons per month.

*Me:* How much would that cost?

*Frank:* Four thousand gallons costs $30.45, and 5,000 costs $36.23. Then when you jump up to 10,000 gallons, that costs $57.86.

*Me:* By the way, where does your water come from?

*Frank:* Lake Rathbun.

*Me:* And those big water towers that I see by the side of the road... are they holding tanks that provide gravity flow down to the customers?

*Frank:* Right. That's where we get our pressure.

*Me:* I've been wondering something for years.

Why don't those tanks freeze up in winter?

*Frank:* Well, we use enough water, so it's either going in or coming out the tank all the time, and our pumps are set up on radio control, so the water's moving all the time. But sometimes they do freeze.

*Me:* Could they freeze so much that the tanks break?

*Frank:* Yup. We've had them split the sides. We just wait 'til spring, wait 'til they thaw out, then go back and weld them up.

I had seen a telephone pedestal on the property near where the mobile home had sat, so I knew that hooking up a phone wouldn't cost any more than it normally would cost in the city. And since electric service had already been run onto the property, I wouldn't have to worry about that expense.

Everything inside me said that the parcel was just what I wanted. The barn, which was in very good condition, was probably worth somewhere between $3,000 and $4,000. And the land itself, with its lush timber and hills and gullies, was beautiful. Finally, the place was very isolated.

The $6,000 that the seller was asking seemed like a fair price, and since I intended to pay cash, and therefore didn't have to wait for financing, I was anxious to buy the property as soon as possible. Because I didn't want to take the chance that a counter offer might cause the seller to change his mind, I decided not to make a counter offer.

Without any misgivings, I called Mr. Waterhouse.

*Me:* I've been out to the property a number of times and I've decided to go ahead and buy it. What do we do next?

*Seller:* Well, I'll call up my attorney and maybe we can meet at his office. You can make a deposit then. What would you prefer, twenty or twenty-five per cent?

*Me:* Uh... well... uh...

*Seller:* When I bought another piece of property awhile ago, the seller wanted twenty-five per cent.

*Me:* Let me talk to my attorney about it.

After hanging up, I called my attorney, who told me that the typical deposit usually ran somewhere between ten and twenty per cent. Since I was knowledgeable about purchase agreements and real estate transactions, we agreed that he wouldn't have to be present when I signed the contract.

Early the next morning I drove down to the seller's attorney's office. Mr. and Mrs. Waterhouse were sitting in a huge leather sofa next to the attorney's desk, and we chatted for a few minutes about the weather before getting down to business.

*Attorney:* What sort of a deposit will you be making?

*Me:* I don't know. What do you think?

*Attorney:* How about $500?

Mr. Waterhouse and I both nodded our agreement. The attorney called in his secretary and told her to type up the contract, and while we were waiting, I used my pen and a notebook to divide $500 by $6,000. The deposit amounted to 8.3 per cent of the sale price.

Mr. Waterhouse said that he had dropped the abstract off at the title company that morning, and that they would try to get it updated within a week or two. After I signed the contract and wrote out a check for $500, we all shook hands and left.

That weekend I attended a farm auction where I bought two

metal road gates for $3.75 each. As soon as I owned the property, I planned to block off the entrance to the property to thwart trespassers. The gates were rusty, but were structurally sound, and I knew that brand new 8-foot gates cost about $40 each. I tied them onto the roof rack of my Datsun and headed down to the property.

During the drive, I started to worry.

*In some ways, the 8-acre parcel was nicer. The creek was beautiful, for one thing. And maybe I should have checked out this 15-acre parcel more thoroughly. I should have talked to all the neighbors.*

I had deliberately not introduced myself to the neighbors. The property was so wonderful, and I wanted it so much, I was afraid that if one of the neighbors had been unfriendly, or maybe even outright nasty, it might have discouraged me from buying the property.

After arriving at the land and storing the gates inside the barn, I decided to take a walk in the woods.

Although it was a hot day, the tree cover completely shaded the ground. On the side of one of the gullies, I came upon a small evergreen tree about eight inches tall. I was surprised it had survived without direct sunlight. I reached down and stroked its green needles with my hand.

"That's all right, little fellow," I said out loud. "Even if we don't get rain, I'll come and water you."

\* \* \* \*

I had told my attorney that I wanted to look at the updated abstract before we went to the closing. Thirteen days after the contract had been signed, I finally got to see the abstract.

I wasn't ready for the surprise it would bring.

CHAPTER THIRTY-TWO

# A SURPRISE EASEMENT

The abstract, which I picked up at my attorney's office, indicated that the first owner had purchased my property, which was then an 80-acre parcel, from the federal government in 1848 for $100.

During the intervening 144-years, the property changed hands thirteen times. In addition to the entries chronicling transfers of title, the abstract also contained references to land contracts, mortgages, taxes, probate matters, and an easement.

The easement was a shock. According to the entry, in 1988 the then owner of the property granted a right-of-way easement to the local rural electric cooperative. The right-of-way was for fifty feet on either side of a line which ran for 800 feet diagonally across a corner of the property. The easement read, in part:

> Owner grants unto cooperative, its successors and assigns, the right, privilege and easement of right-of-way to lay, construct, operate and maintain underground conduit and cable lines for transmitting and distributing electric power, including all wires, cable, handholes, manholes, transformers, transformer enclosures, concrete pads, connection boxes, ground connections, attachments, equipment, accessories and appurtenances desirable in connection therewith, under, upon and across the lands of owner... Cooperative shall have the right to inspect, rebuild,

remove, repair, improve and make such changes, alteration, substitutions and additions in and to its facilities as Cooperative may from time to time deem advisable, including the right to increase or decrease the number of conduits, wires, cables, handholes, manholes, connection boxes, transformers and transformer enclosures. *Cooperative shall at all times have the right to keep the easement clear of all buildings, structures or other obstructions, trees, shrubbery, undergrowth and roots.* [Italics added.] Owner may use the land within the easement for any purpose not inconsistent with the rights hereby granted, provided such use does not interfere with or endanger the construction, operation or maintenance of Cooperative's facilities. For the purpose of constructing, inspecting, maintaining or operating its facilities, Cooperative shall have the right of ingress to and egress from the easement over the lands of Owner adjacent to the easement and lying between public or private roads and the easement, such right to be exercised in such manner as shall occasion the least practicable damage and inconvenience to Owner.

While reading the easement, a feeling of panic built up inside me. The property, I now realized, would not really belong to me, at least not all of it.

What a fool I had been! When I had visited the property, I had noticed that there was an above-ground power line that ran through a corner of the property near the county road. However, it didn't dawn on me that because there was a power line on the property, as well as poles sunk into the ground, there must be an easement. I had seen the power line, but I hadn't thought about its significance.

I got in the car and drove down to the property. When I got

there, I went to the northwest corner and counted the poles. There were three of them. Strung between the poles about twenty feet in the air were two thin power lines. There were no tall trees for about fifteen feet on either side of the poles. The ground wasn't completely bare, however, for there were numerous clusters of bushes and undergrowth.

*Hey, this isn't that bad. The power line is way over here in the corner of the property, right next to the county road. I wouldn't be building anything over here anyway.*

About thirty feet in front of me, a rabbit darted out from behind a tree and ran into a clump of bushes. Wanting to get a closer look at it, I walked towards the bush. Then I noticed the berries. Blackberry bushes, about three feet tall, were growing under the power line. Not all of the berries were ripe, but those that had turned black, tasted wonderful.

After collecting about a quart of the juicy berries, I held my shirt out in front of me to make a basket. Then I walked to the barn, sat down on the ground, and ate them. They were delicious.

*     *     *     *

When I returned home, I called the power company and asked to speak to someone about growing trees on an easement. My call was directed to a fellow named Dan in the customer service department.

> *Me:* The easement says that fifty feet on either side of the power line has to be kept clear of trees and shrubbery.
>
> *Dan:* No, not really. We just need enough room to get our trucks in there.
>
> *Me:* To service the lines?
>
> *Dan:* To trim the trees, mainly. Ten feet on each

side of the line is what we want. And
don't get me wrong. We don't always have
that much. Ten feet is the optimum.

Me: How about if I planted trees in the
easement... a type of tree that wouldn't
grow high, like a dwarf fruit tree?

Dan: Sure, that'd be ok. Our lines can't be
below eighteen feet, so if you want to plant
a tree that's not going to go higher than,
say, fifteen feet, that's fine.

Along with the abstract, my attorney had given me a written
Abstract Of Title opinion. In this letter he said that, after
examining the abstract of title, he found that merchantable title
to the property was held by Thomas Waterhouse and his wife,
subject to the easement that had been granted to the cooperative.

The letter also suggested that I examine the property to see if
there had been any recent improvements. If so, mechanics'
liens* might yet be filed by persons who had furnished labor or
materials for improvements to the property within the last
ninety days.

Finally, he noted that "the correctness of lot area and
boundary rights is not assured by this opinion. In order to
ascertain the correctness of lot area and boundary lines, you
should have the premises surveyed by a qualified engineer."
Because of his earlier statements reassuring me that the fences
constituted the property's boundary lines, I decided not to have
the property surveyed.

The next step was the closing.

---

* A mechanic's lien is a claim that is recorded against a piece of real estate
when work by a contractor has been performed on a building, but has not
been paid for. Such a lien can also be filed by a lumberyard (or other supplier)
that provided materials, in the event the contractor fails to pay the
lumberyard.

CHAPTER THIRTY-THREE

# THE CLOSING

After going to my bank and getting a money order for $5,500, I drove down to the office of the seller's attorney. Five of us were present at the closing: Mr. and Mrs. Waterhouse, the two attorneys, and myself.

The whole process didn't take more than five minutes. The Waterhouses and I signed a warranty deed, which, along with the abstract, was turned over to me. I handed over the money order, and the sellers gave me two checks. One was for $8.80, the amount that I'd have to pay for the revenue stamp at the courthouse. The other check was for $20.71, which represented the amount of property tax that the seller owed, pro-rated up to the day of closing.

I also received a copy of a "Groundwater Hazard Statement." In this document, the seller verified that the property had no solid waste disposal sites, hazardous wastes, underground storage tanks, or wells.

I gave my attorney a check for $200 for his services, and told him that I would prefer to drive down to the Fillmore Courthouse right away and record the deed myself.

After we all shook hands, I asked the seller a few final questions.

> *Me:* Have you removed everything from the property that's yours?

185

*Seller:* Yup.   I went and got those sheets of plywood that were stacked up in the barn, but I left you one old piece of tin. Thought I'd throw it in with the deal. Ha ha ha.

*Me:* Has there ever been a house on that property?

*Seller:* Nope. Just that mobile home for about a year. You know, if I was you, I'd sell the timber. A logger would come in and cut out the bigger trees. Why, you'd get enough to pay for the whole property, almost.

I didn't know anything at that time about the advantages of selectively thinning out a forest, so cutting down my timber seemed like desecration.  After all, the dense forest was one of the most beautiful features of my land.

Anyway, now that the closing was over and the land was legally mine, I was anxious to go down and see how the place made me feel. Would I be satisfied with the property, or would I wish I had continued the search?

## CHAPTER THIRTY-FOUR

# FIRST NIGHT
# ON MY LAND

Out in the street my attorney and I shook hands. "If you run across any other cheap properties," he said, "let me know. You've gotten me thinking that maybe I'd like a place like yours. A place out in the boondocks."

On the way to the land I stopped at the courthouse, where I handed the deed over to the recorder, along with a check for $10 for the recording fee. The clerk stamped the deed with the time and date, then explained that after the deed had been photocopied and the copy filed, I'd receive the original back in the mail.

Then I headed to my property. Along the way I remembered the story that a married couple, friends of mine, had told me about their purchase of a forty-acre farm. The minute their closing was complete they raced to the farm and ran out into one of the fields. Hugging each other and jumping up and down with joy, they yelled out loud at the top of their lungs, "It's ours, it's ours."

I didn't react like that when I got to my property. Instead, I sat down on the ground under one of the big, beautiful oak trees and did nothing. I just sat there in silence.

On that beautiful July day, in the cool shade of that huge tree, I realized that the *hunt* for the property had been exciting, but what I now felt was almost the opposite of excitement.

As I looked at the green moss growing on the side of the tree, and as I heard the wind blowing through the woods, I felt calm, and I felt quietly grateful.

\* \* \* \*

I had brought a pup tent with me, and after laying down a tarpaulin as ground cover, I pitched the tent in the clearing at the back end of the property.

About an hour after dark I crawled inside the tent and got under the blankets. It had been at least thirty-five years since I had slept in a tent, and it made me feel like a teenager again.

As I lay there with the fresh night air cooling my face, I thought of the things I wanted to do the next day. When sleep came, I slept soundly.

At 4:30 A.M. the birds awoke me. I ate the granola and milk I had brought with me and watched the sun come up.

Later that morning I moved the tractor down to the land. I was initially worried that the engine might conk out half way into the trip, so I asked a friend of mine to follow me in his car. My father came along for the ride, and I put all my tools in my friend's trunk, along with an extra battery, a set of battery cables, and a tire pump.

The tractor started right up. As I backed it out of Daryl's shed I noticed that my father looked worried.

*Father:* Don't go too fast.

*Me:* Dad, top speed is only fifteen miles per hour.

*Father:* Still, you better be careful.

Dad's eyesight had gotten so bad that he could barely see, but he could still worry about me.

The trip went smoothly. I had planned my route so as to keep to the gravel roads, since I didn't like the idea of creeping along at fifteen miles per hour on a paved road where cars would be trying to pass me at fifty-five.

I had stuffed a Butterfinger candy bar into my pocket, and half way through the trip I peeled off the wrapper and ate the bar while driving. A wide grin came over my face as I realized I was fulfilling my childhood dream of a tractor and candy bars. At one of the farms I passed by, a farmer was hitching a wagon to a tractor. He looked up and waved at me, and I waved back.

As I backed the tractor into the barn, Dad continued his earlier conversation.

*Father:* I worry about you and that tractor.

*Me:* Come on, Dad. I'll be careful.

*Father:* It might turn over on you some day.

*Me:* Hey, Dad. This is a lot less crazy than some of the dangerous things you've done in your life.

Dad just shook his head, slowly, from side to side.

A few weeks later something happened which proved that Dad's fears had been justified.

CHAPTER THIRTY-FIVE

# A BRUSH WITH DEATH

Months before I bought my tractor, I read books and magazine articles about tractor safety. Even though I knew that you shouldn't attach a pulled object to the wrong spot on the tractor, this didn't prevent me from making a very stupid mistake. It happened about two weeks after I purchased my property, when I decided one day to get rid of an unwanted tree.

Although most of my fifteen acres are covered with timber, about half an acre is cleared. This ground, which abuts the county road, has a deep layer of fertile topsoil covered with grass. The tract would make a great vegetable garden some day, so I decided not to let the clearing revert back to forest.

In the middle of the clearing stood a hawthorn tree. It wasn't a big tree, only about ten feet tall. However, the large thorns on its limbs could easily pierce the front tires of a tractor, and if I ever wanted to plow and plant the ground, the tree would be in the way. Better to get rid of it now while it was small.

Using the tractor to pull it up by the roots wouldn't be too difficult, I reasoned. The tree consisted of three small trunks, each about four inches in diameter, which joined together just below ground level.

My plan was to remove each of the trunks, one at a time, by pulling them out with a chain. I took one end of a log chain and wrapped it twice around one of the trunks. Then I attached the other end of the chain to the rear axle of the tractor.

That was the mistake. I should have attached the chain to the tractor's drawbar.*

However, a few weeks earlier I had removed the drawbar to make room on the back of the tractor for a jerry-built platform I had fashioned out of metal and wood. The platform allowed me to pick up cement blocks from one spot on the property and transport them to the barn.

If I had thought about what I was doing, I would have realized how dangerous it was. By attaching the chain to the axle rather than the drawbar, I was directing the tree's resistance to a point relatively high up on the tractor, making it more likely to tip over.

If a tractor is hooked up to a very heavy object (or to something like a tree), it may be easier for the tractor to slowly tip itself over backwards than to move the heavy object (or the tree). If this happens, the driver can be crushed to death under the tractor.

I climbed up onto the tractor seat and put the transmission in first gear. Then I let up on the clutch. As the tractor inched forward, the chain bit into the tree.

I turned my head backwards to see what was happening. The tree bent slightly. The engine started to strain under the load, and as the governor sent more gas into the carburetor, the muffler roared louder.

The tree didn't give. Instead, the front of the tractor started to rise off the ground. By the time I realized what was happening, the front wheels were two feet up in the air and still rising.

As I felt myself tipping backwards, instinctively I grabbed hold of the steering wheel more tightly and jammed my left foot down on the clutch pedal.

* The drawbar is a sturdy metal bar protruding from the back of the tractor. It is the drawbar to which you attach such pulled objects as wagons and plows.

I got the clutch disengaged only half way before my muddy boot slipped off the pedal. With a jerk, the clutch reengaged, and the front of the tractor started rising again. I was terrified.

I thrust out my left foot once more towards the clutch, but the tractor had tilted up so much that I had almost slipped off the seat. I could no longer reach the pedal.

Suddenly, the tractor fell forward and the front wheels hit the ground with a loud thump. I quickly disengaged the clutch and shut off the motor. I remained seated on the tractor, my body shaking. If the tractor had gone back much further, it would have toppled over onto me.

But why had it stopped? When I walked back to the tree, I discovered that a link in the chain had snapped.

I cut the tree down a few days later with a hand saw. Not only was this a safer method of solving the problem, but I was now anxious to get started on a new project: creating a comfortable place to sleep.

CHAPTER THIRTY-SIX

# A PLACE TO SLEEP

*Me:* Do you think you might be interested in
selling the building?

I was referring to a 12x16-foot structure that I had seen by the
side of the road. Although it was located roughly twenty miles
from my property, I was hoping to buy it cheap, then move it to
my land. After tracking down the owner, who lived in a
different county, I had called him on the phone.

*Owner:* Yes, we might be interested in selling. We
were going to use it for a vegetable stand,
but we really don't need it that bad. So if
you're interested... I don't know, we've got
quite a bit of time and lumber in it. You
know, even these little sheds you see
advertised seem to cost quite a bit, but we
were thinking somewhere around $2,000
for it.

*Me:* That's quite a bit more than what I was
thinking of.

*Owner:* Well, it's got a lot of lumber in it, and you
know what the lumber prices are these
days. But if you think that's steep, then
make us an offer on it.

Although the building wasn't new, it certainly was pretty.

Rectangular in shape and with a simple gable roof, it had a door and four windows, two of which had been covered with shutters.

The structure was covered with wood siding hung vertically, and I could easily imagine it nestled amongst the trees on my property. I could furnish it with a bed and a wood burning stove, and even in the dead of winter, with the snow falling and the wind blowing, I could spend a cozy night deep in the quiet of my woods.

However, I wasn't going to pay $2,000 for it. I had been thinking about offering $400 or $500, but after the owner mentioned his price, I decided it was pointless to make a counter offer.

Of course, moving a building onto my property wasn't the only way of acquiring a cabin. I had originally thought of erecting a small building myself. One way would be to buy an old barn or shed, tear it down and transfer the lumber to my property, then build a small cabin.

I spent days mulling over this idea, and I even made rough sketches of a 12x12-foot structure. The problem was, I really didn't have the time to tear down a building, piece by piece, then reconstruct it on my land.

I also considered building a log cabin. There were hundreds of long, straight trees on my property, and although cutting them down would be a lot of work, it might take less time than tearing down and reconstructing an old building. But after reading a book by someone who had constructed his own log house, I decided that I didn't have the time or stamina for such a project. In addition to tree-felling and bark removal, each log would have to be dragged to the cabin site, notched at each end, then lifted into place and chinked.

Then I got the idea to buy and assemble one of the garage kits that I saw advertised by the large lumber companies.

After assembling a kit, it wouldn't take much extra work, I reasoned, to insulate and finish off the inside and turn it into a one or two-room cottage. The problem with this scheme, though, was price. Even the cheapest garage kits cost between $1,600 and $2,000, which was much more than I wanted to spend.

I next considered buying a used mobile home. Although I'd have to hire someone who had the proper permits and equipment to move the home, there wouldn't be much work for me to do. I found a number of trailers for sale in the $800 to $1,000 range, but they were all pretty crummy. Most of them suffered from leaky roofs that hadn't been repaired properly, and each time I stepped into one of these cheap homes I was confronted with an unpleasant aroma. The odor seemed like a combination of mildew, urine, and over-cooked fish, onions, and broccoli. I didn't want to acquire a home that gave me the creeps every time I walked into it.

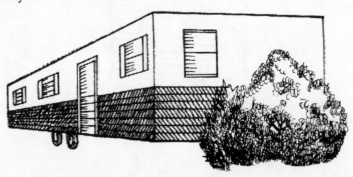

I also looked at a couple of 12-foot camper trailers. The first one, which the seller wanted $450 for, had a jagged hole in the roof through which I could see the sky, and the wall and floor sections underneath the hole had rotted out. Although I could replace the damaged wood, I'd never be able to get rid of the damp, moldy smell.

The second camper was selling for $850, and it was pretty clean inside. It had a bed, table, kitchen, and closets, but after sitting down on the bed for a few minutes trying to imagine myself spending weekends inside the unit, I realized it was just too small. Although the outside dimensions were 7x12 feet, the amount of unused floor space measured only 4x5 feet. As my Dad had often quipped, "That's not even enough room to allow you to change your mind."

Then, one day when I was backing the tractor into the barn, I thought of another alternative. Why not build a room on top of the barn? Excited by the idea, I climbed up into the space between the ceiling joists and the roof rafters and tried to imagine what a room up there would look like.

I could almost stand up straight at the middle of the roof, so there might be enough space, especially if I built a dormer whose roof sloped upwards from the highest point of the existing roof.

There would be a number of advantages in building on top of the barn. I wouldn't have to go to the time and expense of creating a foundation, and since the barn's interior would act as a basement, the new room might be easier to heat than would a cabin on the ground.

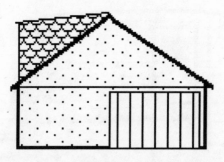

But the more I thought about it, the less I liked the idea. For one thing, I kept the tractor in the barn, and whenever I started the engine up, the barn quickly filled up with exhaust and gasoline fumes. If I built a room on top of the barn, those fumes might seep up into the living space.

Also, I liked the looks of the barn the way it was. It was a simple structure, similar to some of the barns and sheds on neighboring farms. If I built a dormer on it, it might end up looking out of place. I decided not to alter it.

So, for almost a year, whenever I wanted to spend the night at the property, I'd sleep in my pup tent on the ground. That was fun the first few times, but as fall turned to winter, it became obvious that, to really make use of the land, I needed a permanent, heated, sleeping cabin.

The solution turned out to be surprisingly inexpensive.

## CHAPTER THIRTY-SEVEN

# A TINY HOUSE

Whenever I drove anywhere during the following months, I kept my eyes open for small barns, old mobile homes, and camper trailers. Eventually, I hoped, I'd find something that would be just right.

One day in August, while driving down one of the paved roads in Fillmore County, I noticed a small building sitting in a pasture. The structure looked like a garage, but it sat in the middle of the field, about 800 feet from the road. There were no other buildings nearby. The garage was shaded by a couple of trees, and although I couldn't see much more than its outline, it appeared that one of the trees had fallen on a corner of the building's roof.

It didn't look as if much damage had been done, and since the owner hadn't removed the tree, maybe he didn't want the building.

*My property is only about seven miles away, so the garage probably wouldn't be too hard to move.*

During the next few weeks I made a point of driving down that road whenever I got the chance. Each time I passed by, I looked to see if the tree had been removed. It was always there.

One day, seeing a man and a pickup truck in the pasture next to the garage, I stopped my car and walked into the field. At a small clearing in the back of the pasture, a middle-aged farmer was burning a pile of trash. He wasn't wearing a hat, which seemed strange, since the temperature was in the 90s and there was a blazing noonday sun.

When I told him I might be interested in buying the garage and moving it, he said that I was welcome to take a look at it, but that he doubted whether it would be suitable.

After opening the door and examining the inside of the building, I saw what he had meant. The roof had been leaking for a long time, possibly years, and many of the roof rafters had rotted out. Using my pocket knife to check the soundness of the rest of the garage, I discovered that many of the ceiling and wall joists were also soft with rot. Even if the garage could be moved in its present condition, which seemed unlikely, I'd probably end up having to replace a third of the structure's framing.

I walked back to the farmer and told him that he had been right. I *was* looking for something in a little better condition.

*Farmer:* Well, I got a couple other buildings. Small ones, on a different property. Take a look at them. See what you think.

*Me:* How far away are they?

*Farmer:* Over near Four Corners.

*Me:* Where's that?

He paused, then looked me in the eyes.

*Farmer:* You're not from around here, are you?

After I admitted that I wasn't, he gave me directions on how to get there. But he kept referring to local landmarks that I wasn't familiar with, such as "the Yoder farm," and "old man Thompson's place."

*Me:* Could you draw me a map?

There was another pause, and I couldn't tell from the

expression on his face whether he was annoyed or amused.

*Farmer:* Heck! I've done enough damage for the day. I'll drive over there and you follow.

We drove about eight miles to an old farmstead. When we got there, the farmer told me he had purchased the farm from the estate of an elderly widower who had recently died. The buildings, he said, were of no use to him. He had bought the place only for its 340 tillable acres.

The farmhouse, which looked as if it had been built around the turn of the century, had apparently been vacant for years. The side porch had collapsed, and the front and back doors were wide open. In front of the house, weeds came up to my waist.

Behind the house was a barn, as well as two smaller outbuildings. The barn, which was two and a half stories high, was too big to interest me. The smaller buildings looked promising, though. Each was a little smaller than a one-car garage, and both had wood siding that had been painted white.

I looked first at the building with a tin roof. Since the structure had no windows, it was really just a shed. On its north side was a small wooden door, not more than five feet high. I lifted the old wrought-iron latch that was attached to the door, then stepped inside. The building had a dirt floor and no ceiling. In fact, there weren't even any ceiling joists. The structure's framing was so flimsy that I realized I'd have to do a lot of bracing just to jack it up, let alone move it.

While the farmer went to the barn to check on some machinery, I looked at the other small building which sat directly behind the farmhouse. Rectangular in shape, it had a gable roof, three windows, and a door. The exterior of the building was finished with horizontal wood siding. Unlike the shed, this structure looked like a tiny house.

Even though the door was ajar, I had difficulty stepping inside because of all the junk on the floor. There were rolls of old roofing paper, two wooden wagon tongues, wash tubs, and piles of lumber and scrap metal in various shapes and sizes. Hanging from nails on the wall were old harnesses and coils of barbed wire.

However, this building had a wood floor, and there was a ceiling of 2-inch-wide tongue and groove boards. The interior walls hadn't been finished off, but that made it easy to inspect the building's stick frame construction. At each corner was a 4x4, and between these posts 2x4 studs were spaced about every sixteen inches.

Standing in the middle of the structure, I tried to imagine how the place would look if all the junk were removed.

*What would this room be like if it had a potbelly stove and a bed? Would I feel comfortable sleeping here?*

It was hard to tell, since the overall impression, at that moment, was one of junk and dust. However, the building had potential. The three windows provided a lot of light, and the place already had a ceiling and a floor.

Stepping outside, I took a tape measure and jotted down the

structure's dimensions: ten feet wide by fourteen feet long. Kneeling down on the ground at the base of the building, I pulled up some of the weeds to see what sort of foundation the structure had.

A 6-inch-high wall of concrete was visible between the ground and the lowest board of siding, and after examining all four sides of the structure, I found that there was a poured foundation running completely around the building. However, there were no access holes or gaps in the concrete, and this was frustrating. It meant that I wasn't able to look underneath the building to determine what sort of joists or beams had been used for support.

Next, I looked at the roof, which was covered with asphalt shingles. Even without a ladder, it was easy to see that the roof on the west side of the building was in bad shape. Some of the shingles were missing, and others were bent up or torn.

*If I could crawl up under the roof, maybe I could determine if the leaks have done any structural damage.*

Stepping inside again, I noticed a hole in the ceiling about one foot square that had been covered up with a piece of tin. After getting a flashlight from my car, I piled some of the lumber on top of two of the wash tubs, and by using this as a step, I was able to push back the tin and pull myself up into the attic.

White stains on the underside of the west roof indicated that water *had* gotten inside, but when I used my pocket knife to probe the wood, I couldn't find any soft spots. The water apparently hadn't done any real damage. I did notice, however, that there was a circular hole in the roof that was now covered with shingles. The hole was about eight inches in diameter, and was above (and directly in line with) the hole in the ceiling through which I had made my entry. There must have been a stove in the building at one time.

After climbing down from the attic, I went outside and sat down on the grass. As I looked at the little building, brightly white in the noonday sun, I came to the conclusion that it was not only good looking, it was charming.

I wanted that building.

*Wait a minute, though. Will I be able to move it all the way to my property? After all, I'm not even sure how to lift it off its foundation.*

As usual, though, my feelings won out over my intellectual misgivings, and I decided to buy the little structure.

After thinking about it for a few minutes, I decided that I'd be willing to spend $500 for the building. However, I felt that I should offer only $90. If the farmer didn't accept my offer, I'd have room to dicker. I decided, though, that before I made the offer, I'd see if I could get *him* to mention a price.

I walked over to the barn where I found the farmer changing the oil in a tractor.

*Me:* I'm interested in the building that's closest to the farmhouse. Do you have any idea how much you want for it?

He looked down at the floor and took a moment before answering.

*Farmer:* A hundred dollars.

*Me:* I was going to offer $90, so I guess we were thinking in the same range. $100 is fine with me. Is it all right if I take a few months before I move it?

*Farmer:* That's ok. Take your time.

That suited me fine since I planned to move the building myself.

## CHAPTER THIRTY-EIGHT

# JACKING THE BUILDING

Eighteen years earlier I had spent three summer months working for a house mover in upstate New York. During that time I had helped move a number of houses, some barns, and a Pizza Hut building.

The house mover had long lengths of steel I-beams, expensive hydraulic jacks, as well as specially built trailers and wheel sets that could be attached to the I-beams. Most of my work had consisted of loading and unloading hundreds of railroad ties, and stacking them, one on top of the other, Lincoln-log-style, to create cribs in the basements of the buildings to be moved.

After four cribs had been built in a basement, we'd knock out holes in the foundation, then slide two I-beams through the holes and underneath the house. Next we'd put a jack on top of each crib, position the I-beams over the jacks, and slowly lift up the building.

I had never been involved, however, in lifting or moving a small building. Also crucial was the fact that, although I now owned lots of hand tools, I didn't have any special house moving equipment. The only heavy-duty lifting device I owned was a simple hydraulic floor jack, the kind that garage mechanics use.

I was optimistic, though, that I could figure out some way to accomplish the move. My plan was to rent a trailer, jack the building onto it, and drive it to my property. It'd be fun.

The first step was to do something about the leaky roof. I bought a large roll of plastic and draped it over the roof, fastening it with boards and nails so the wind wouldn't blow it off.

The next step was to break a hole in the foundation to see what was underneath. Using a 10-pound sledge hammer, I delivered a powerful blow to the concrete. The blow didn't even make a crack. I swung a few more times, also without effect. The only thing the blows were doing was sending painful shock waves into my hands and arms.

Since I wasn't getting anywhere with the foundation, I decided to remove a few of the lower pieces of siding. I had heard that it was possible to lift a small building by inserting beams into holes in the siding.

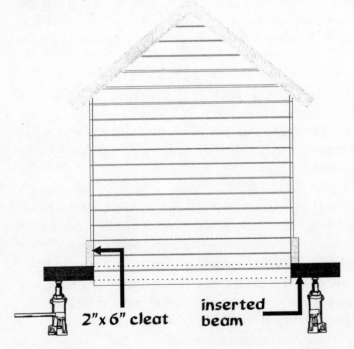

2" x 6" cleat      inserted beam

With the beams in place, you would nail 2x6 cleats to the exposed wall studs, just above the beams. The beams, being longer than the width of the building, would stick out through the walls, and you could put jacks under the ends of the beams. As you started jacking, the beams would rise, pushing up against the 2x6 cleats, and the structure would lift.

My building was sheathed in lap-and-groove siding, which, of course, had originally been installed lower course first, with each succeeding upper course overlapping the course below it.

I wanted to remove only two or three of the lowest boards. The problem was that, since each board's upper edge was snugly wedged into the next board's grove, and since the nails holding the boards were firmly embedded, any one board couldn't be pulled cleanly away from the building.

Nevertheless, I gave it a try. From inside the building, I used a hammer to whack at the lowest piece of siding, right next to a stud. Instead of dislodging the board, the blow split the board in two. I decided to call it a day.

On the way home, I started to worry. Not only couldn't I penetrate the foundation, I wasn't even able to remove a piece of siding without destroying it. Maybe the move was going to be more difficult than I had anticipated.

That night, when I told a friend that I was going to move a building, she said I should talk to Floyd, an 88-year-old friend of hers who was a retired house mover. I immediately gave him a call.

> *Me:* I'm planning to move a small building, 10x14 feet, and I wonder if I could ask you some questions.
>
> *Floyd:* Has it got a floor on it?

*Me:* Yes. I guess that makes it more difficult.

*Floyd:* No, it makes it easier, because you have floor joists to lift it with. Where do you got to take it, over the highway?

*Me:* No, just over gravel roads. About fourteen miles.

*Floyd:* How tall is it?

*Me:* Not that tall. Maybe twelve, fourteen feet. I don't know.

*Floyd:* You have to know exactly how tall the building sits, from the ground to the peak of the roof. I'm thinking about wires.

My mind flashed back eighteen years to when the outfit I was working for was moving a house down a paved country road. The building was only a story and a half high, but the movers, in order to save money, hadn't paid the utility company to raise any of the wires along the road. Each time we came to an overhead wire, one of the movers, who was riding on the peak of the building's roof, would take a lawn rake in his hands, grab hold of the wires with the tines of the rake, and lift the wires up five or six feet so the house could pass under.

*Floyd:* If your building, once it's sitting on the trailer, is over fifteen feet high, you'll need to get the power company to raise each wire along your route. That can get mighty expensive.

Realizing that I had lots of questions for Floyd, I made an appointment to meet him in person to continue our conversation. The next morning we talked for two hours, sitting in lawn chairs in his back yard. For many years he had been involved in the business of moving buildings and huge machinery, and he possessed a wealth of information about the subject. As the sun warmed our faces, I took notes while he patiently explained every step that I'd have to follow.

If I kept hammering away at the foundation with the sledge, Floyd said, the concrete would eventually give way. I'd need to remove the bottom course of siding in order to unscrew the nuts from the bolts that held the sills to the foundation. I'd never get anywhere hammering the siding off from the inside. Instead, I'd have to remove the nails from the boards with a nail puller. I could buy one at the hardware store.

I should borrow some bridge planks and slide them under the floor joists. Put rollers under the planks, he said, then use a winch and chains to slide the building onto a trailer.

If I pulled the building over even a small distance of paved road, I'd need a permit from the state Department of Transportation. However, if my route was confined to gravel roads, I wouldn't need a permit, provided that the building was no more than fifteen feet high.

The following Saturday, after packing my Datsun with jacks, tools, lumber, and a ladder, I drove the twenty-five miles to where my building sat. It was a cool but sunny day, and as I unloaded my tools, I was glad to be outdoors.

Following Floyd's advice, I measured the height of the structure. The peak of the roof was 11 feet 9 inches above the foundation. That meant that, in order to stay below the 15-foot limit, I'd have to find a trailer that was no more than 3 feet 3 inches high.

I decided that, before using the sledge hammer on the foundation again, I'd take a shovel and dig away some of the earth from the outside of the foundation. I was curious to see how far down into the ground the concrete went. After digging a hole about two feet wide, I discovered that the foundation extended fourteen inches below ground level. It wasn't surprising that my earlier whack with the sledge hadn't been successful.

With heavy leather gloves on my hands, I started swinging the sledge at the foundation. For the first six blows, nothing happened. Then, on the seventh swing, a crack appeared in the foundation. After four more blows, I had dislodged a small piece of the concrete.

Now that the concrete had been breached, the process went quicker. It took about six blows to break off each succeeding piece of concrete. Some pieces were as small as oranges, others as large as footballs.

Since I wasn't used to such strenuous labor, I found the work exhausting. It took me about an hour of work to break a 12-inch-wide gap in the foundation.

By lying on the ground and shining a flashlight into the hole, I could see into the cavity. The floor joists, which ran perpendicular to the building's longer walls, were bigger than I had expected. Reaching in with a tape measure, I discovered that the joists were 2x8s. For a building only ten feet wide, I had expected 2x6s.

More surprising, though, was the fact that the bottoms of the joists were not resting on the sills. The lower corner of each joist had been notched out, leaving only the top 3¾ inches of the beam as support.

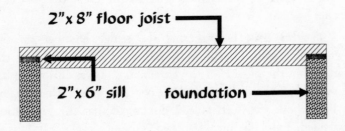

210

This weird positioning of the joists was more than just a curiosity. It created a problem. Because the bottom of the joists extended almost four inches below the top of the foundation, there was very little dead space between the bottom of the joists and the ground. In spots, the clearance was only two inches, not anywhere near enough for bridge planks, rollers, and jacks. Maybe I'd have to return to my original idea of raising the building by inserting long poles through the sides of the structure.

Abandoning this problem for the moment, I decided to try out my new nail puller.

After a few strikes with a hammer, the puller's claw was imbedded under the head of the nail, and I could pry the nail out. (The nail puller is really just a special kind of crowbar, one that allows you to grab hold of a nail that is flush with the wood surface.) It took almost an hour to remove the three bottom courses of boards from each of the four sides of the building.

With the boards off, I could examine the condition of the sills. I was pleased to find that most of the wood was sound. Only under the door, where water had penetrated, was there a portion of rotten sill.

On each side of the building there were three bolts sticking up through the sills. The twelve bolts, which were embedded in the concrete, held the sills to the foundation. Each bolt had a large nut on it. The bolts were rusty, but after spraying them with penetrating oil, I was able to remove the nuts with a crescent wrench.

That night I called Floyd. When I told him about the limited amount of clearance between the ground and the floor joists, he said to use a Handyman jack.*

* Popular with farmers and contractors, the tool is sometimes called a Hi-Lift jack.

This tool, which has a long lifting arm, would allow me to get a toe-hold under the sills of the building.

Considering the size of the building, he said, I could get by with two of these jacks. Start out with them on one side of the building. Then, when that side is raised six inches or so, fill the gap with 2x6s, then move the jacks to the other side. Of course, I'd first have to break out four holes in the foundation (two holes on each side) to allow the arms of the jacks to reach under the sills.

After making a number of trips to the farm, it became obvious that I needed something more than my Datsun sedan for the project. I needed to transport lots of wood, including bridge planks and railroad ties. And once the building was raised, I'd need a vehicle that could haul a trailer with a building on it.

Initially, I considered using my tractor for the move. However, since I'd want to ease the building forward without any jerky movements, a vehicle with an automatic transmission would be best. After a couple of weeks of looking, I bought a 1975 Chevy half-ton 4-wheel-drive pickup truck for $450. It was in pretty bad shape, but it ran.

I also looked into renting a car-hauling trailer. I discovered that the Ryder Company would rent me one for $30 a day, whereas U-Haul charged $45 for theirs. Both trailers were eight feet wide and about thirty-two inches high. While at the rental companies, I drew a diagram of each trailer, complete with measurements for ground clearance, wheelbase, length, etc.

I was able to borrow a Hi-Lift jack, but since I needed two of them, I bought a second one, new, for $44. Floyd had said to position each jack at a point on the sill directly underneath one of the floor joists. That way, the greatest amount of weight would be directly over the jack, and the sill would be less likely to split.

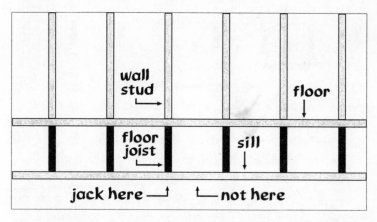

It took and hour and a half to break holes in the foundation for the jacks. It was hot, sweaty work. Although none of the foundation had been reinforced with steel, its thickness made it difficult to break up. By the time I was finished, I was exhausted.

Even with all the bolts loose and the holes for the jacks created, there was one last thing I had to do before trying to raise the structure. The walls had to be braced to prevent twisting.

After cleaning out all the junk from inside the building, I took 2x4s and nailed them, diagonally, to the inside surfaces of the wall studs. I used double-headed nails so the boards could be removed easily after the move.

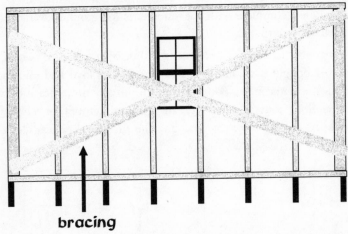

**bracing**

Up until now, none of the work I had done on the building had been dangerous. Now, however, it was time to start jacking up the structure. Raising any building, even a small one, can be quite hazardous. Since I was working alone, and because the farm was uninhabited, there would be no one to help me if I got in trouble.

I pictured the building being slowly raised, then slipping off its jacks and pinning my arm against the foundation. I remembered reading about a man whose leg had been crushed under a felled tree. To extricate himself and save his life, he took a saw and cut off his leg.

I decided to leave word with a friend of mine who was a deputy sheriff. I drew him a map showing where the farm was located, and each time I went down to the farm I called him and put him on notice. If I didn't phone him by 9 p.m. that night, I said, it meant I was in trouble and that he should come looking for me.

I was now ready to lift the building. Positioning the lips of the jacks under the sills, I pushed down on the lifting arm of one of the jacks. I had to press down with all my weight. Slowly, the lifting arm gave way. I heard a creaking noise from the building, and, crouching down on my hands and knees to get a good look at that corner of the building, I noticed that there was now an eighth of an inch gap between the foundation and the sill.

I let out a yell. It was working!

Using the second jack, I raised the other corner of that side of the building. Next, I inserted shims into the gap, then went back and forth between both jacks, raising each a click at a time, until there was enough of a gap for me to slide a 2x6 plank into the cavity.

Moving the jacks to the other side of the building, I repeated the process. After a couple of hours, the building had been lifted about eight inches and was resting on four layers of 2x6s.

Although I would have to eventually raise the building a total of about three feet, I didn't trust the stability of a higher stack of 2x6s, so I decided to stop jacking for the day.

Now that the building was off the foundation, I could get a good look at the underside of the structure. The 2x8 floor joists appeared to be in perfect condition. Using a tape measure to check the distance between the two foundation walls on the longer sides of the building, I got a reading of 8 feet 8 inches.

*Hey, wouldn't one of those trailers fit in here? If I could back a trailer right under the building, I wouldn't have to put planks and rollers in here in order to slide the building onto the trailer.*

Rainy weather put a stop to my work for two weeks, but during that time I was able to buy sixteen railroad ties. I paid only $75 for the lot, but I had to borrow a trailer and drive forty miles to pick them up.

When the rain stopped, I continued jacking the building up until there was three feet of clearance between the ground and

215

the bottom of the floor joists.

I had to use the sledge hammer to remove enough of the foundation at each corner of the building so cribs could be built at those points. At each corner I built a crib consisting of four railroad ties and assorted scraps of lumber. None of the cribbing could protrude into the cavity under the building, since I had decided to back the trailer directly under the building.

Next, I broke away all of the foundation on the south end of the building. There needed to be a flat stretch of ground at that end of the structure in order to back the trailer under.

Although the building was now ready, there was one final thing to do before the move.

CHAPTER THIRTY-NINE

# THE BIG MOVE

I now had to choose a route. The most direct line would take me over two stretches of paved roads, and would thus require a permit from the Iowa Department of Transportation. Instead, I chose a course that ran over only gravel roads. It was about two miles longer, and for one mile actually went in the opposite direction from my land. But this route would allow me to make the move without having to obtain a DOT permit.

I decided that, before the actual move took place, I should drive over the route one time to make sure there would be no unexpected problems, and to check the height of all overhead lines.

I knew that it would be impossible to hold fifteen feet of metal tape measure straight up in the air under each power line, so I decided to cut a measuring pole that was exactly fifteen feet long. Then I got the idea to use my body's 6 feet 2 inches as part of the measurement. That way, I could get by with a pole only 8 feet 10 inches high. The shorter pole would be lighter to handle, and would ride in the pickup truck's bed without falling out or snapping in two.

The pole worked perfectly. When I got to the first overhead wire, which was a power line running to a farmhouse half a mile down the route, I got out of my truck and stood under the wire. Taking off my hat, I raised the pole and held it on top of my head. The top of the pole was at least five feet below the wire.

I went through the same procedure at every wire along the route. Only one wire was too low. When I held up my measuring pole, the top of the pole was at least two feet above the wire. The line, probably a home-made installation, ran from a barn on one side of the road to a windmill on the other side.

Some of the blades on the windmill were missing, and the unit wasn't turning, so it was unlikely that there would be power in the line. It could easily be lifted to let the building pass under. However, I wanted to avoid the chance of a confrontation with the property owner, so I looked at the map and plotted a slight deviation in the route to avoid that farmstead.

With the test run complete, the only remaining task was to prepare the spot on my property where the building was to go.

For weeks I had been trying to decide where I was going to put the building. If my plans had been to live on the property year-round, I might have chosen a location close to the county road. The hookup for rural water would be relatively cheap at that location, and during the snowy months of winter, the chance of getting the car or truck stuck would be minimized.

But since I was planning to use the property mainly for weekend visits, the desirability of seclusion overweighed convenience. I decided to put the building down near the barn, at a spot about 600 feet away from the county road, deep in my woods. Although I might not be able to get my car down there during the rainy season in spring, when the road turned muddy, at least my truck could probably get through. And if the truck couldn't, there was always the tractor.

At a point about fifty feet down the land from the barn, I used my chain saw to cut down five trees for a clearing. The open space would be just big enough for the building, but the remaining trees would still be close enough to the structure to provide shade during the summer.

After cutting the trees, I stopped by to see Daryl, the farmer I had become friends with after he offered to store my tractor before I bought my land. When I told him that I had bought a building for $100, he offered to help move it. Up until now, I had been able to do everything by myself, including foundation removal, jacking and bracing. The actual move, however, would require help.

I needed drivers for two extra vehicles, one in front and one behind the moving building, in order to give notice to passing traffic. Additionally, I worried about something going wrong. If the building shifted once it was on the trailer, or if the building started to fall apart, I wouldn't be able to leave it in the middle of the road, or even on the side of the road. I'd have to immediately correct whatever problems came up, and for that, I'd need help.

I decided to make the move on a Sunday, since there would be less traffic on the road that day. The night before the move, I picked up a trailer that a friend of Daryl's had agreed to rent me.

After pulling it to the farm, I spent a frustrating half hour getting the trailer positioned properly under the building. The trailer was exactly eight feet wide, which meant that there were only four inches clearance on each side within the foundation. Between the top of the trailer and the bottom of the building there were four inches of clearance.

Lowering the building was just the opposite of raising it. Using the jacks to support one side of the structure, I removed one layer of cribbing. Then I switched to the other side and repeated the process.

On the day of the move, Daryl showed up with three of his neighbors, all of whom were farmers. The fact that all of them had experience moving small buildings reassured me. They helped me chain the sills to the trailer to prevent the building from shifting its position. But when I showed them the map and pointed out the route, they balked.

>*Daryl:* Why don't you use the hard surface road? It's shorter.

>*Me:* That road is a state highway, and to be legal, I'd need a DOT permit.

>*Daryl:* Technically, yes. But this is just a small summer kitchen, and farmers move this type of building all the time without permits. Nothing happens.

>*Me:* You guys have lived here all your life, and everybody knows you. Maybe you could get away with it. But if a state trooper drove by and caught me, I bet he'd make me park it. Being Sunday, I couldn't get a permit.

>*Daryl:* You're worrying too much.

>*Me:* I don't want to take the chance.

I didn't give in, and Daryl didn't say anything more. But I made a mental note to ask him later what a summer kitchen was.

Now we were ready. I got into the pickup truck, engaged the low end of the 4-wheel drive, and started the motor. I was glad that the truck had an automatic transmission because I didn't want to jerk the building during the drive. The automatic transmission would allow me to start off very, very, slowly.

With my foot on the brake pedal to prevent even a slight forward lurch, I put the transmission in low and gave the engine some gas. When I let up on the brake, we moved slowly forward.

*It's moving! It's working!*

I was so excited that I felt like letting out a yell, but I restrained myself. I didn't want Daryl and his friends to think I was silly.

After inching along in a straight line until the trailer was clear of the foundation, I turned sharply towards the farm's driveway. The farmhouse stood on a hill about thirty feet higher than the county road, and as I eased the building down the inclined driveway, I was tense.

Eighteen years earlier, the house mover I was working for had inadvertently destroyed part of a barn we had been moving. On that day, while the driver of the truck was pulling the barn down a slight hill, he had carelessly applied his brakes too quickly. Although he had been going only about ten miles per hour, the sudden stop shifted the barn on its trailer. I remember hearing wood splinter, and watching helplessly as one corner of the barn collapsed to the ground.

But this day, as I eased the load onto the county road, all I heard was the smooth hum of the truck's engine.

As soon as we were on the gravel road, I increased the speed to five miles per hour. Floyd, the house mover, had told me I could safely go as fast as twenty-five miles per hour, but I didn't dare. The road was rough in spots, and I worried that the constant jarring might dislodge the building.

At the first overhead wire, I slowed down and stopped just before the building reached the line. Even though I had measured the height of the line two days earlier, I knew that it would be disastrous if the roof snagged the wire. Only after getting out of the truck and seeing that there was a good five feet of clearance was I satisfied.

After a few miles of driving, five miles per hour seemed awfully slow, so I eased it up to ten. Nothing bad happened, so I tried fifteen miles per hour.

Daryl was driving his pickup in front of me, about 400 feet ahead, and after about three miles into our route, a car came towards us. Daryl motioned the driver to pull off the road into a driveway that led to a cornfield. Although the county road was wide enough for a car to pass by the house, Daryl had suggested that I keep to the middle of the road, since the sides of gravel roads were often fairly soft. The trailer-house combination was top heavy, and what we didn't need was for one side of the trailer to sink down abruptly.

At one spot along the route, we had to cross a paved state highway. Daryl walked down the highway in one direction about 400 feet, while one of his friends walked in the other direction. As I eased the truck across the pavement, a car came speeding down the highway. Daryl waved his hands above his head and the car came to a stop. I was glad I wasn't trying to make the move alone.

At one of the farmhouses we passed, two boys, about ten years old, were playing ball in the front yard. Seeing us coming down the road, they stopped their game, stood motionless, and stared at us. Then one of them yelled out, "That's illegal!"

The trip took about an hour and a half, but went without any problems. Throughout the whole fourteen mile route, we met only two cars and a truck.

At my property, I turned sharply from the county road into my driveway, but got only half way through the gate before I was yelled to a halt by Daryl. The trailer hadn't straightened out completely from the turn, and the back of the building wasn't going to clear the right-hand gate post.

I had to jockey back and forth a number of times before the building could get through the gate. On the drive down my lane to the barn, we had to stop three times to pull back tree limbs to clear a path for the building's roof.

When we reached the clearing that I had cut the day before, I pulled the building into the trees, and after another series of back-and-forth maneuvers, we got the structure positioned just the way I wanted it. After raising the building off the trailer with the jacks, we used the railroad ties to build four cribs to support the structure, one at each corner.

Although the move was now complete, and the building was no longer in danger, there was one last challenge. There wasn't a wide enough path through the woods in front of the building to get the truck and trailer out, and we no longer could back out over the same ground we had entered, since the building now blocked our exit.

I had known, on the previous day when I had cut the trees, that we'd have to take down more trees in order to extricate the truck and trailer, but I had decided to postpone further cutting until the last minute.

After some discussion, we decided to unhitch the trailer from the truck and pull the trailer out, backwards, from underneath the building. We used Daryl's truck and a chain to do that.

Now, only the truck needed to be extricated from the woods. After considering a number of possible routes, we found a path that required only three small trees to be felled.

At 4 P.M. the five of us sat down for a snack of soda pop and corn chips. As I sat there, in the quiet of the towering trees, I remembered the phrase that Daryl had used to describe the building. I asked him what a summer kitchen was.

Years ago, he said, when meals were cooked over a wood stove in the kitchen of a house, a small structure was often built outside the back door. The out building would have a cooking stove, and during the hot summer months, the family's meals would be cooked in that "summer kitchen." In that way, the main house, where the meals were eaten, would remain cooler.

My new building, originally a summer kitchen, had now become my cabin in the woods.

## Chapter Forty

# ONE MORE DREAM

It's a Saturday morning in October and I'm rushing through a few last-minute chores at home. I'm frustrated at not being able to head out to the property immediately.

As I back my truck out the driveway and head down the street, I let out a deep breath and the muscles in my body begin to relax.

At the property, I unlock the gate and drive down to the barn. The leaves on the trees, which were a dark green just a month ago, have turned red, yellow and brown. Although the air is cold, the sun is out and feels warm on my face.

After attaching a rotary mower to the back of the Farmall, I spend the next two hours clearing out brush and small trees from the flat ground next to the county road. It's more fun than driving a bumper car in an amusement park.

At noon I sit down on the ground and rest my back against a huge oak tree at the northwest edge of the property. As I munch on an avocado sandwich I've brought from home, I look out over the valley and watch a tractor plowing the ground on a farm two miles away.

I return to the barn and use a crowbar and hammer to pry apart some shipping pallets I've salvaged from an alley in Springfield. It's useless work, since I don't have any immediate need for the wood, but pulling out the nails is relaxing.

In fact, just being here is relaxing. There are no projects that *have* to be done. No lawns to mow, no house to paint. It's the perfect place to unwind and to daydream.

*It sure would be great to have a pond. I could take a swim whenever I wanted.*

Any one of the gullies could be turned into a pond. All I'd have to do is build a dam. But it would probably cost three thousand dollars, maybe more, to hire someone to come in with earth moving equipment to create the dam.

I remember the auction I attended a few weeks ago where a bulldozer sold for $2,500. Maybe I could buy one, build a dam myself, then sell the bulldozer for almost as much as I paid for it.

Silly dream? Maybe, but...

# APPENDIX

## Finding Sellers Without Using a Broker

Listed below are various methods of locating potential sellers without having to rely on real estate brokers. Before you try these techniques, contact a number of brokers and visit as many of their properties as you can. You may get lucky and discover that one of their listings is a real bargain. But more importantly, only by learning what the prices are for listed property in your area will you be able to recognize a bargain when you start hunting for acreages on your own.

- ▶ Drive down rural roads looking for abandoned or neglected farmsteads (pages 46-48).

- ▶ Stop farmers you see along the road and ask if they know of land for sale (page 49).

- ▶ Offer a reward (a finder's fee) for information about available land (page 51).

- ▶ Post "land wanted" signs (page 41).

- ▶ Attend (or join) a rural church and tell members you're looking for property (page 50).

- ▶ Go to land auctions (pages 79-81).

- ▶ Ask people at auctions if they know of property for sale (page 49). Do this not only at land auctions, but also at any sales attended by rural residents, such as auctions of livestock, farm machinery, household goods, etc.

- ▶ Print up circulars and attach them to windshields at country auctions and other gatherings (page 50).

- ▶ Investigate the properties that will be auctioned off by the county for unpaid taxes. (pages 84-86).

► Use a boat to find desirable parcels bordering rivers or lakes (pages 38-45)

► Study plat books to locate small parcels (page 76). Topographical maps are also useful (page 40).

► Visit the county courthouse and ask tax assessors (and other county officials) if they know of land for sale (page 51).

► Rent country property and let it be known that you're looking for a parcel to buy (page 50).

► Use barbers (or hair dressers) in rural towns and ask them for leads (page 51).

► Ask bankers if they have any foreclosed property for sale (page 51).

► Leave your name and telephone number at coffee shops, hardware and grocery stores, agricultural co-ops, farm machinery dealers, etc. (page 50).

► Ask town supervisors, sheriff's deputies, attorneys and land surveyors if they know of land for sale (page 51).

► Find out if surplus government land is up for sale in your area (pages 82-83).

► Read classified newspaper advertisements (pages 35-37).

► Place your own newspaper advertisements (pages 13 and 53). This is the technique I found most productive. In fact, by placing multiple ads in a number of small-town newspapers, I ended up with so many responses that I had to write out a list of questions to ask each caller so I could concentrate on the best prospects (page 58).

# INDEX

"This fascinating book will help you find and buy rural property at a bargain price... Even if you're not thinking of buying rural land, sharing Turner's search is time well spent. On my scale of one to 10, this excellent book rates a 10."

— **Robert J. Bruss,** real estate broker, attorney, and nationally syndicated real estate writer

"The key word here is cheap, since if you have enough money, a broker can find you something nice even in Orange County. The trick is to avoid brokers and get out in the sticks... A modest, quirky book, well written and entertaining..."

— **John Mort,** *Booklist*

"This book will grip your attention as tightly as a novel, but it's a true story... and a highly educational one for anyone looking for land to buy."

— *Countryside & Small Stock Journal*

## ABOUT THE AUTHOR

Ralph C. Turner, who is frugal to the point of not being ashamed of retrieving used lumber from his neighbors' trash cans, is always on the lookout for a bargain. In 1986, when he wanted to buy his first computer, he spurned expensive IBMs and Macs for a low-priced Atari ST. He got addicted to computing, and when he was laid off from his salaried job as an editor, he tried to support himself as a free-lance writer for computer magazines. He then authored three top-selling computer books which earned him the nickname, "Mr. Atari." A graduate of San Francisco State College and San Francisco Law School, he now lives in Southeast Iowa where he enjoys writing in the secluded cabin on his country land, and pulling felled trees out of the woods with his antique tractor.